This Nail Art Design Log Book belongs to:

____

DEDICATION

This Nail Art Design Planner is dedicated to all the nail art designers out there who love to plan out nail designs, and document their findings in the process.

You are my inspiration for producing books and I'm honored to be a part of keeping all of your nail design notes and records organized.

How to use this Nail Art Design Planner:

This useful nail art design planner is a must-have for anyone that loves to paint nails! You will love this easy to use journal to track and record all your nail design activities.

Each interior page includes space to record & track the following:

1. Design Name - Write down the name of the nail design.
2. Nail Design Sketchpad - Use this space to sketch out new nail art designs.
3. Description - Stay on task using the space to write out the description of each design.
4. Color Palette - Record and Track the color choices of each design.
5. Details and Patterns - Use this space to list out details of each design.
6. Additional Notes - Space to write out any thoughts, ideas of your nail artwork.

If you are new to the world of nail art design or have been at it for a while, this nail artwork planner is a must have! Can make a great useful gift for anyone that loves to plan out nail art designs!

Have Fun!

DESIGN NAME .... DATE ....

NAIL DESIGN	DESCRIPTION
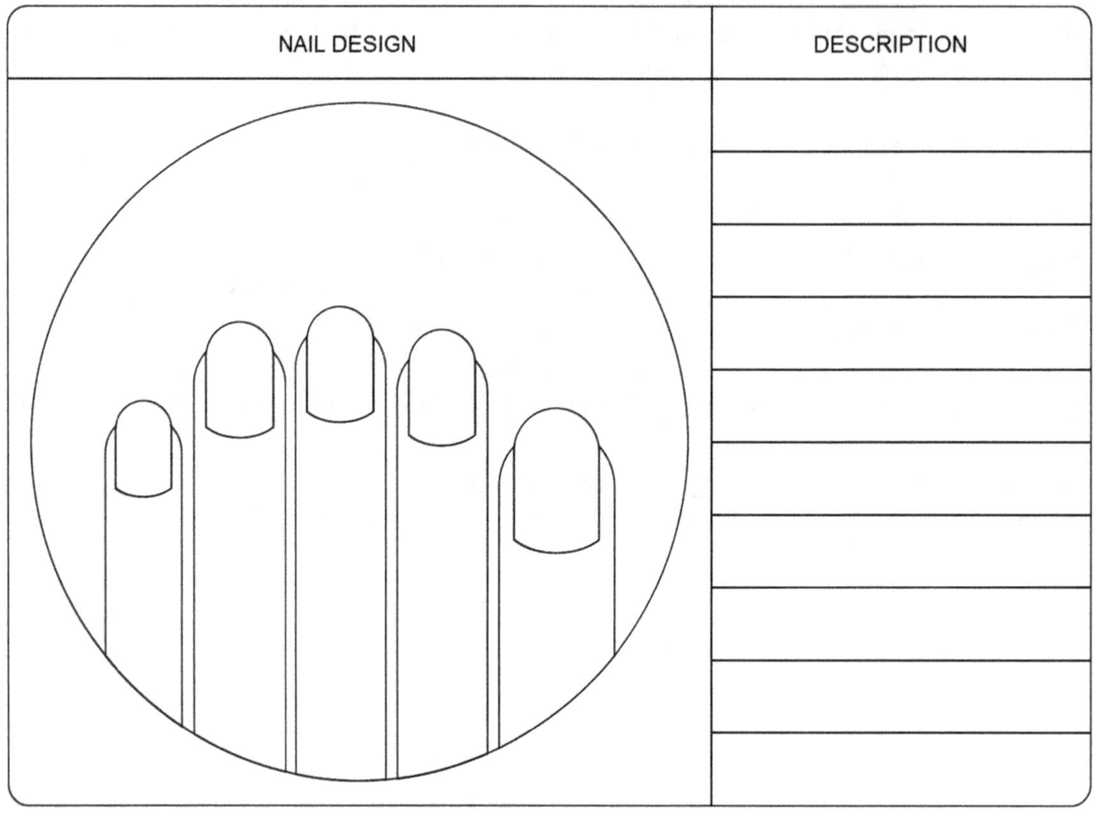	

COLOR PALETTE

1	2	3	4	5	6	7	8

NR	COLOR	BRAND
1		
2		
3		
4		
5		
6		
7		
8		

DETAILS & PATTERNS

ADDITIONAL NOTES

DESIGN NAME .... DATE ....

NAIL DESIGN	DESCRIPTION
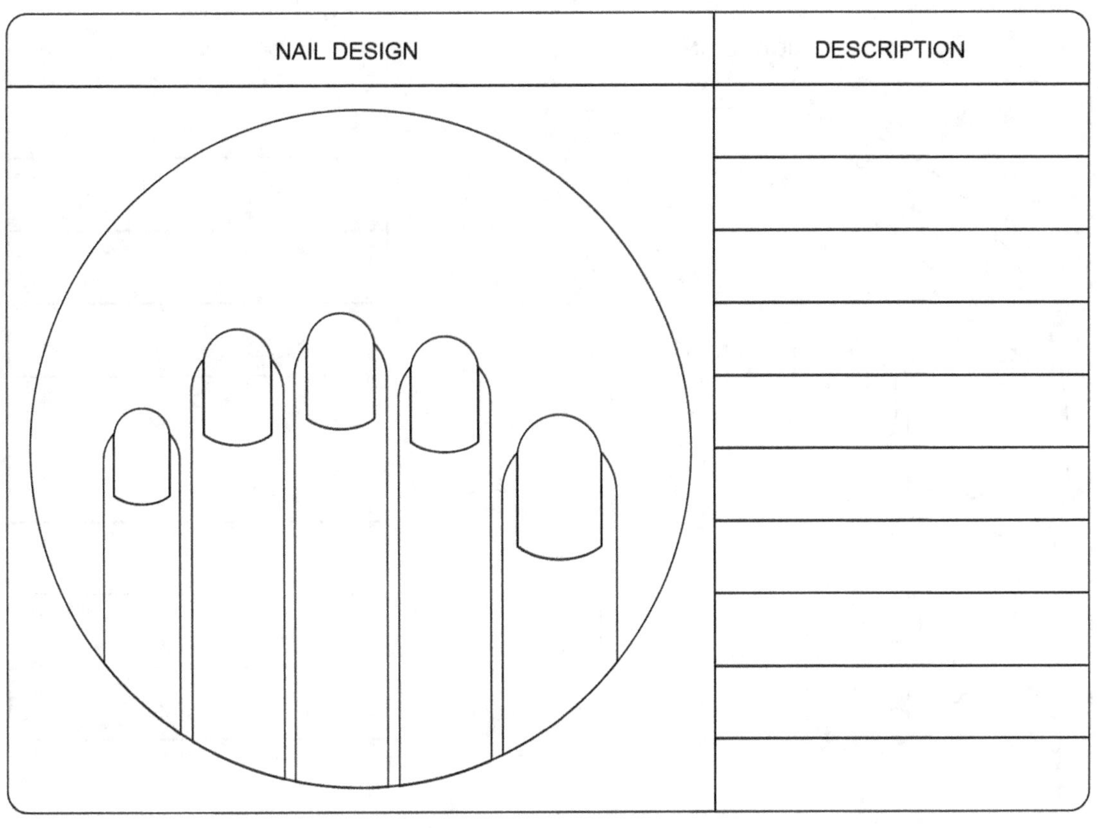	

COLOR PALETTE							
1	2	3	4	5	6	7	8

NR	COLOR	BRAND
1		
2		
3		
4		
5		
6		
7		
8		

DETAILS & PATTERNS

ADDITIONAL NOTES

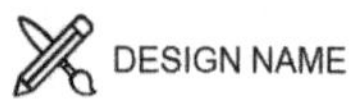
DESIGN NAME ....

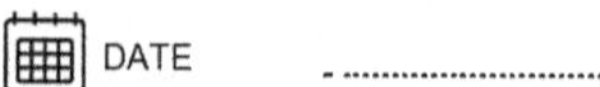
DATE ....

NAIL DESIGN	DESCRIPTION

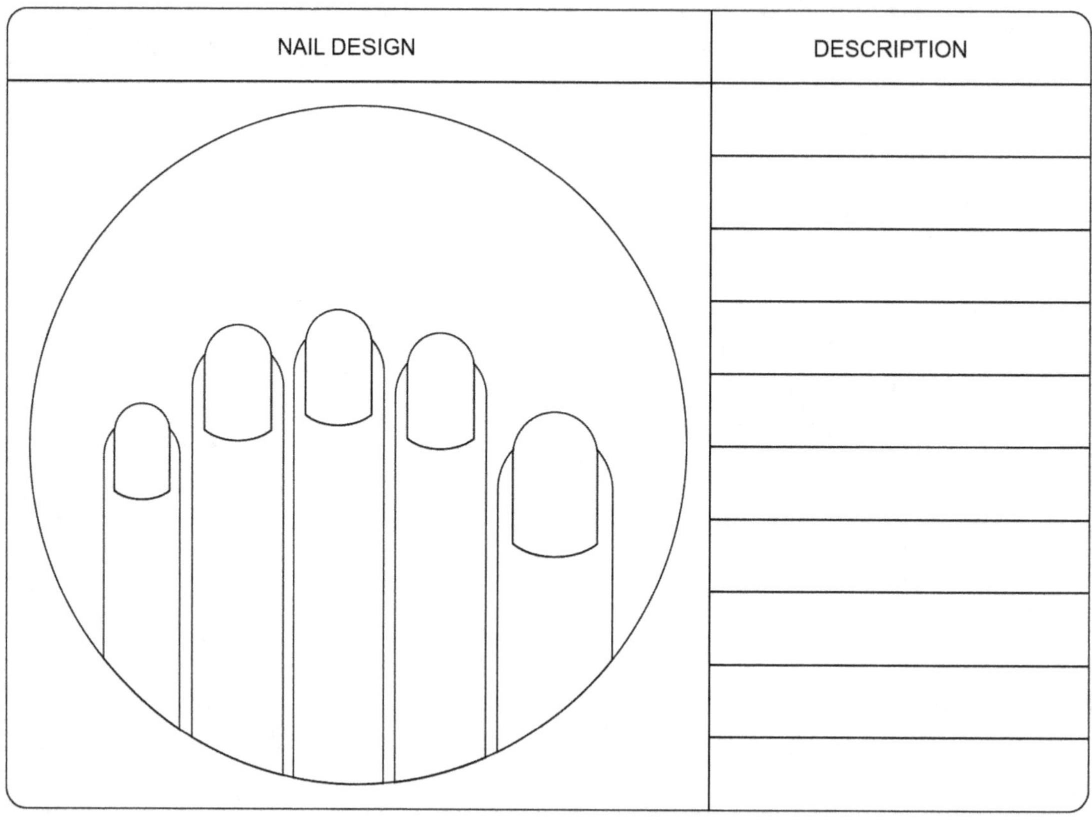

COLOR PALETTE

1	2	3	4	5	6	7	8

NR	COLOR	BRAND
1		
2		
3		
4		
5		
6		
7		
8		

DETAILS & PATTERNS

ADDITIONAL NOTES

DESIGN NAME .... DATE ....

NAIL DESIGN	DESCRIPTION
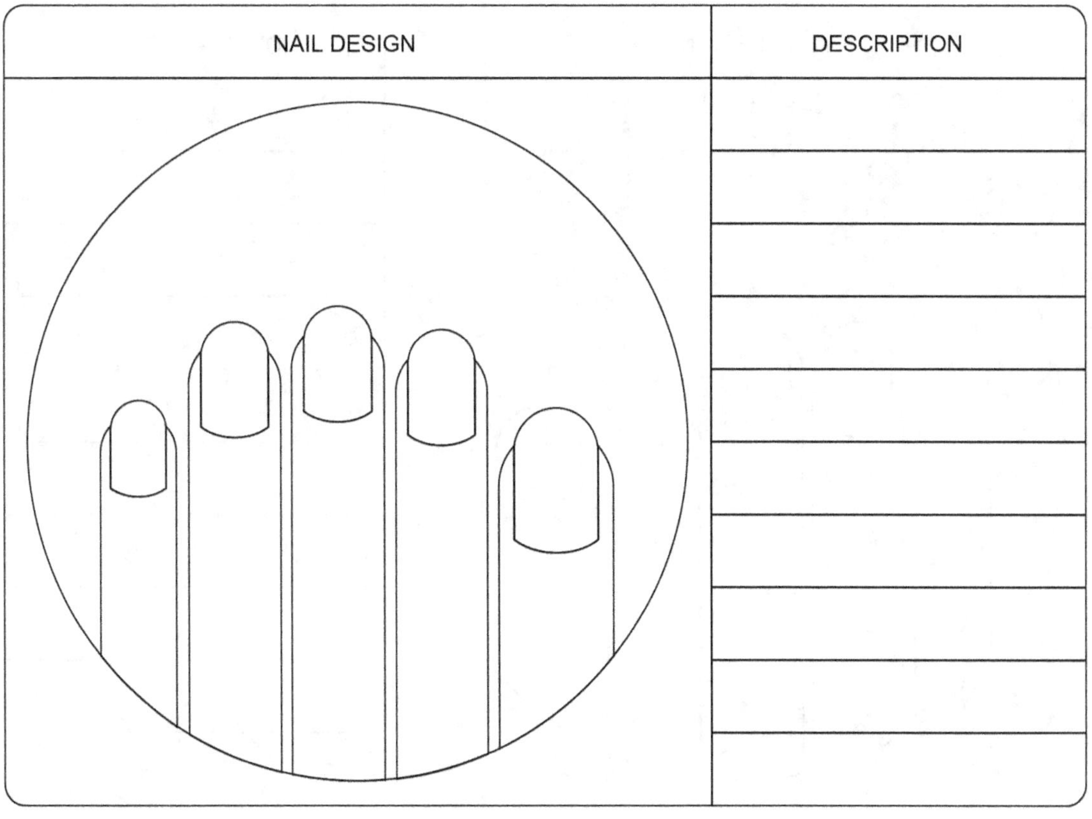	

COLOR PALETTE							
1	2	3	4	5	6	7	8

NR	COLOR	BRAND
1		
2		
3		
4		
5		
6		
7		
8		

DETAILS & PATTERNS

ADDITIONAL NOTES

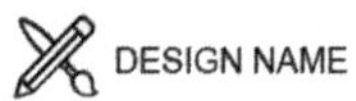
DESIGN NAME ....

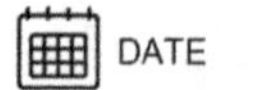
DATE ....

NAIL DESIGN	DESCRIPTION
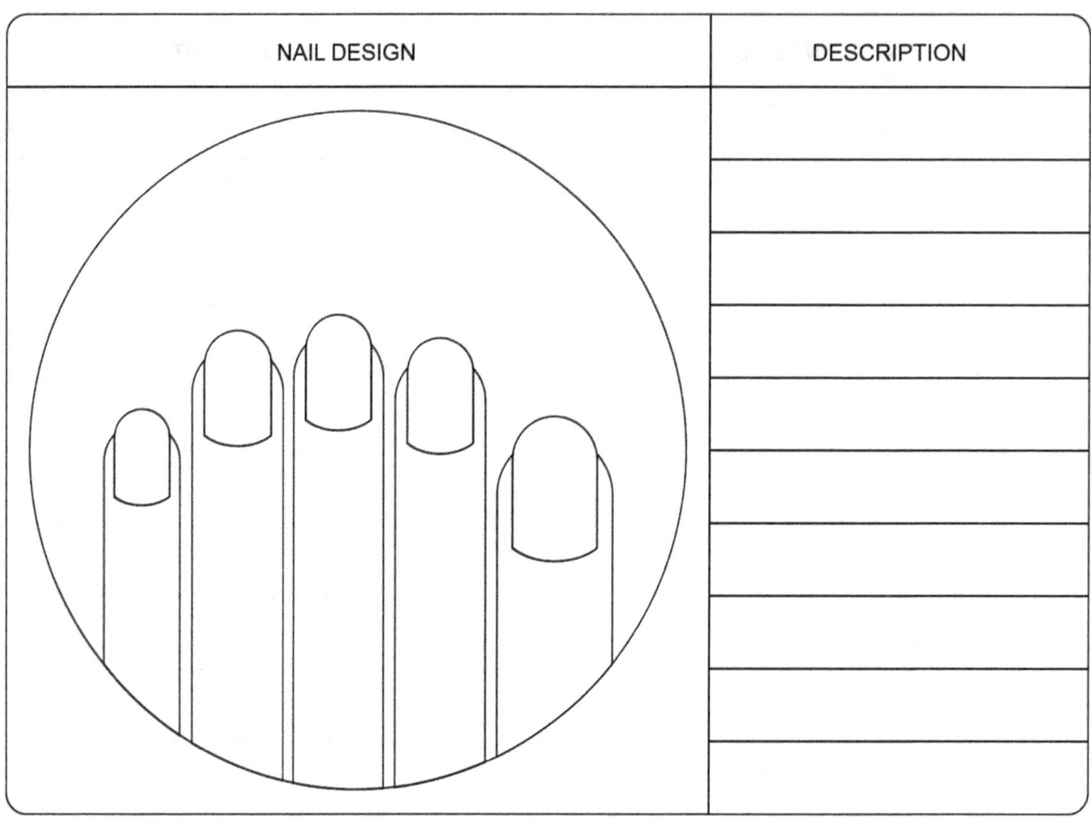	

COLOR PALETTE

1	2	3	4	5	6	7	8

NR	COLOR	BRAND
1		
2		
3		
4		
5		
6		
7		
8		

DETAILS & PATTERNS

ADDITIONAL NOTES

DESIGN NAME .... DATE ....

NAIL DESIGN	DESCRIPTION

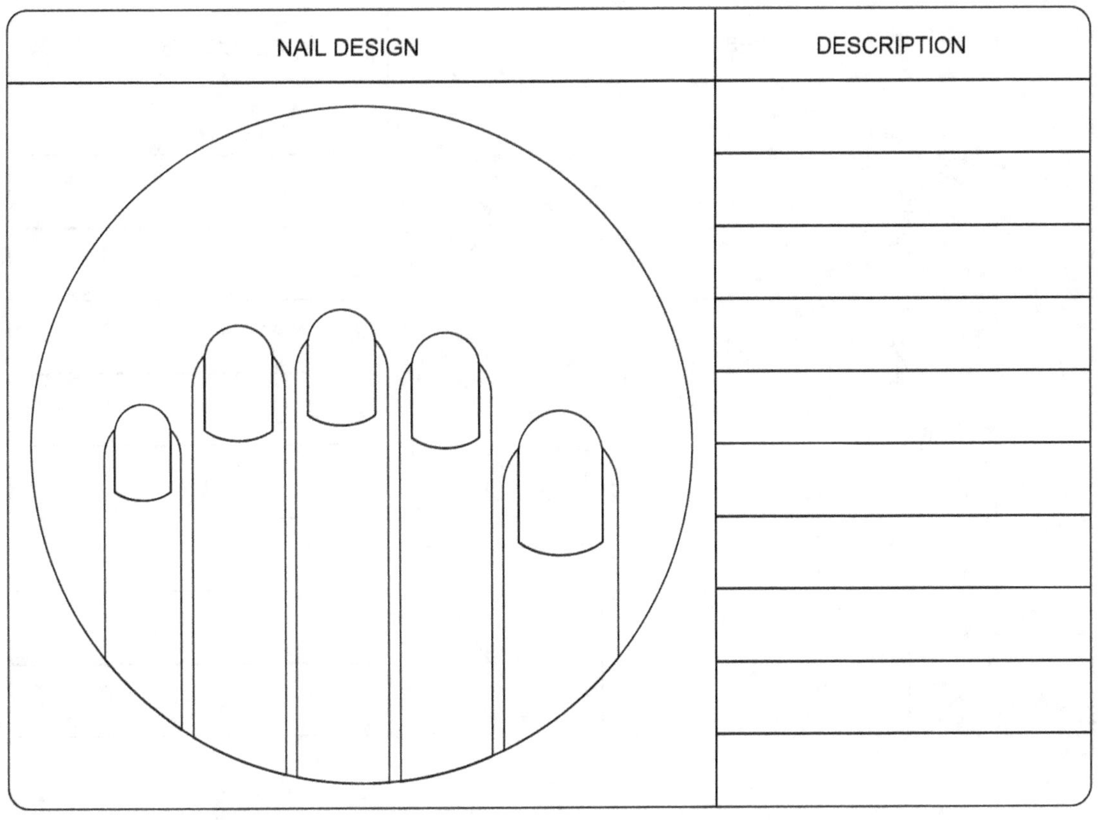

COLOR PALETTE

1	2	3	4	5	6	7	8

NR	COLOR	BRAND
1		
2		
3		
4		
5		
6		
7		
8		

DETAILS & PATTERNS

ADDITIONAL NOTES

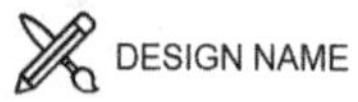
DESIGN NAME ....

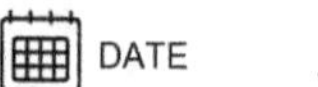
DATE ....

NAIL DESIGN	DESCRIPTION
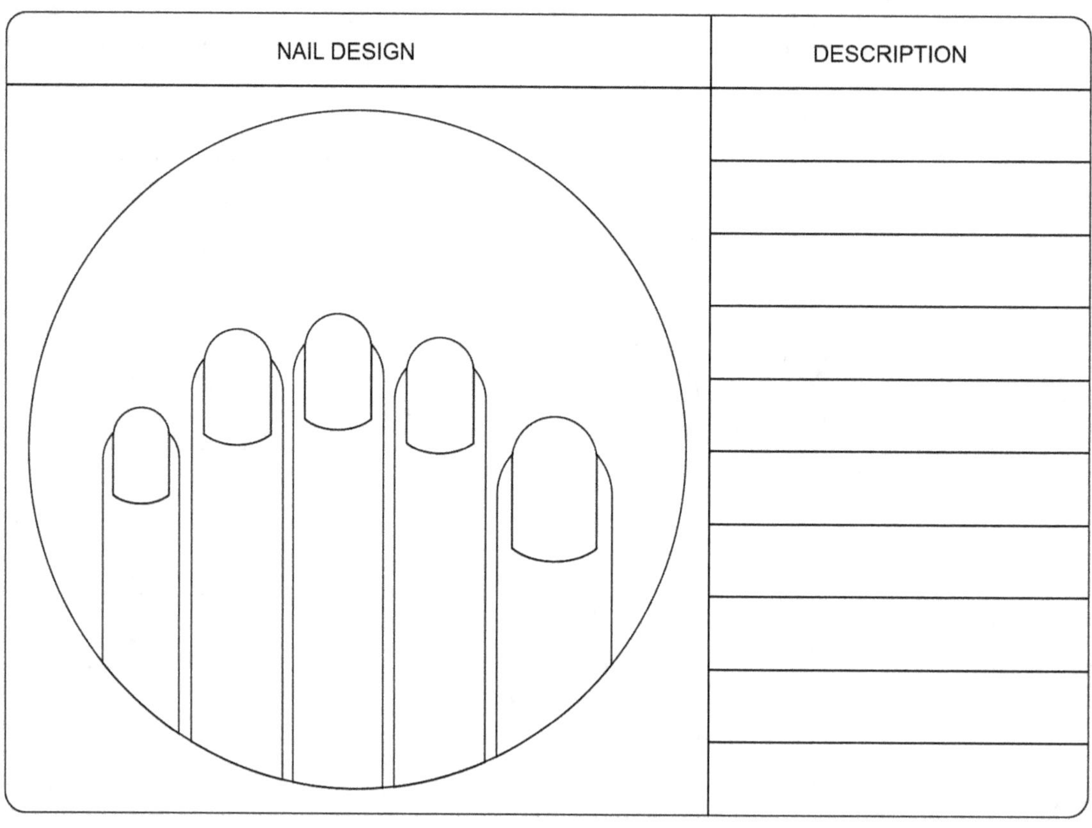	

COLOR PALETTE							
1	2	3	4	5	6	7	8

NR	COLOR	BRAND
1		
2		
3		
4		
5		
6		
7		
8		

DETAILS & PATTERNS

ADDITIONAL NOTES

DESIGN NAME .... DATE ....

NAIL DESIGN	DESCRIPTION
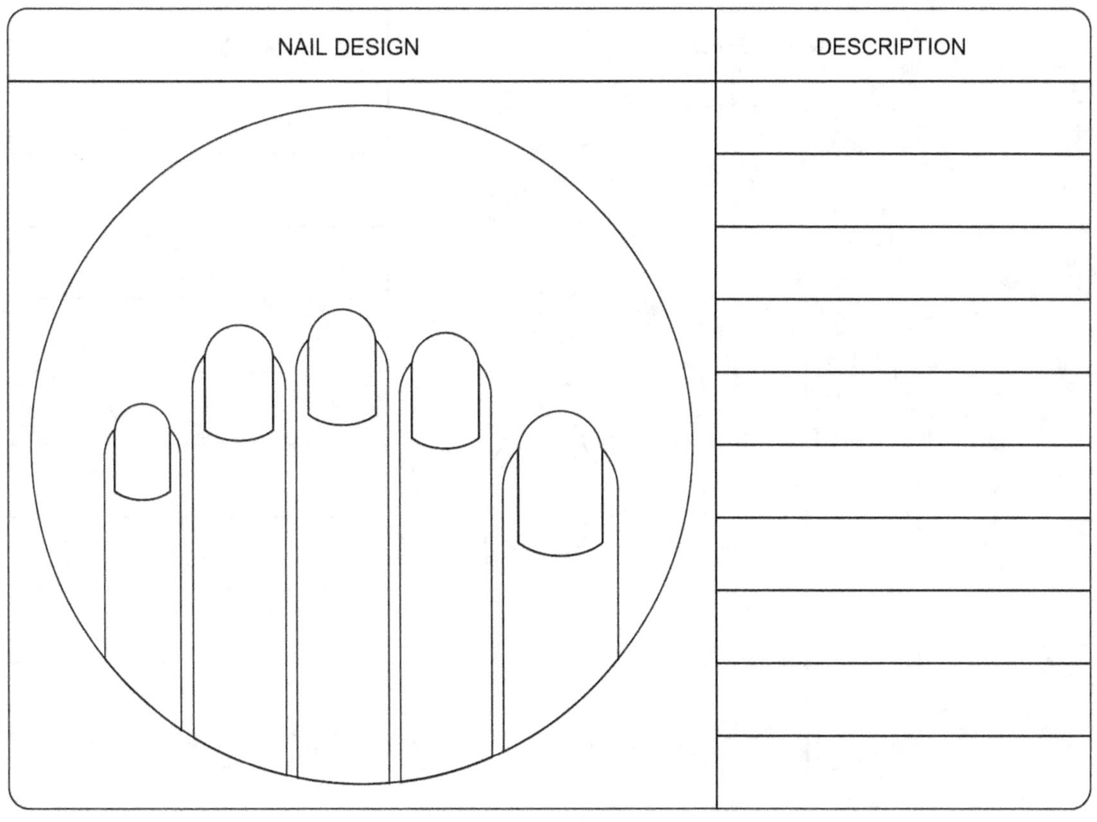	

COLOR PALETTE

1	2	3	4	5	6	7	8

NR	COLOR	BRAND
1		
2		
3		
4		
5		
6		
7		
8		

DETAILS & PATTERNS

ADDITIONAL NOTES

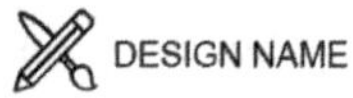 DESIGN NAME ....

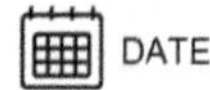 DATE ....

NAIL DESIGN	DESCRIPTION
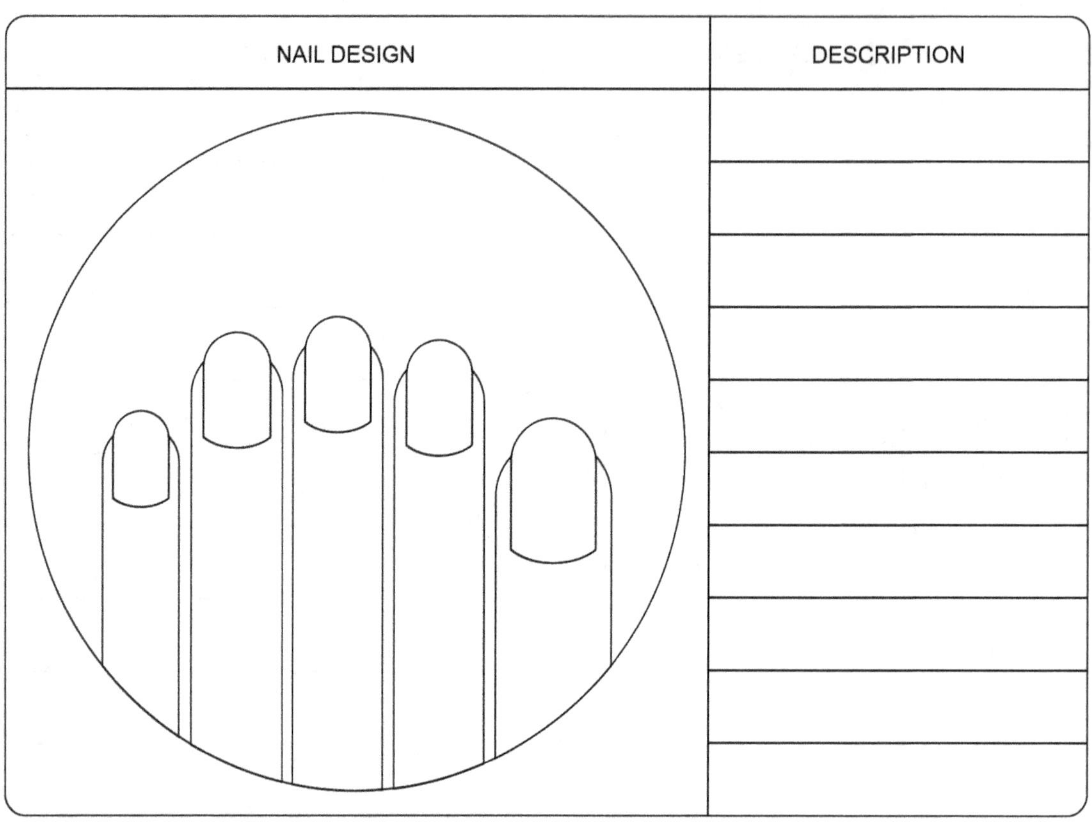	

COLOR PALETTE							
1	2	3	4	5	6	7	8

NR	COLOR	BRAND
1		
2		
3		
4		
5		
6		
7		
8		

DETAILS & PATTERNS

ADDITIONAL NOTES

DESIGN NAME .... DATE ....

NAIL DESIGN	DESCRIPTION
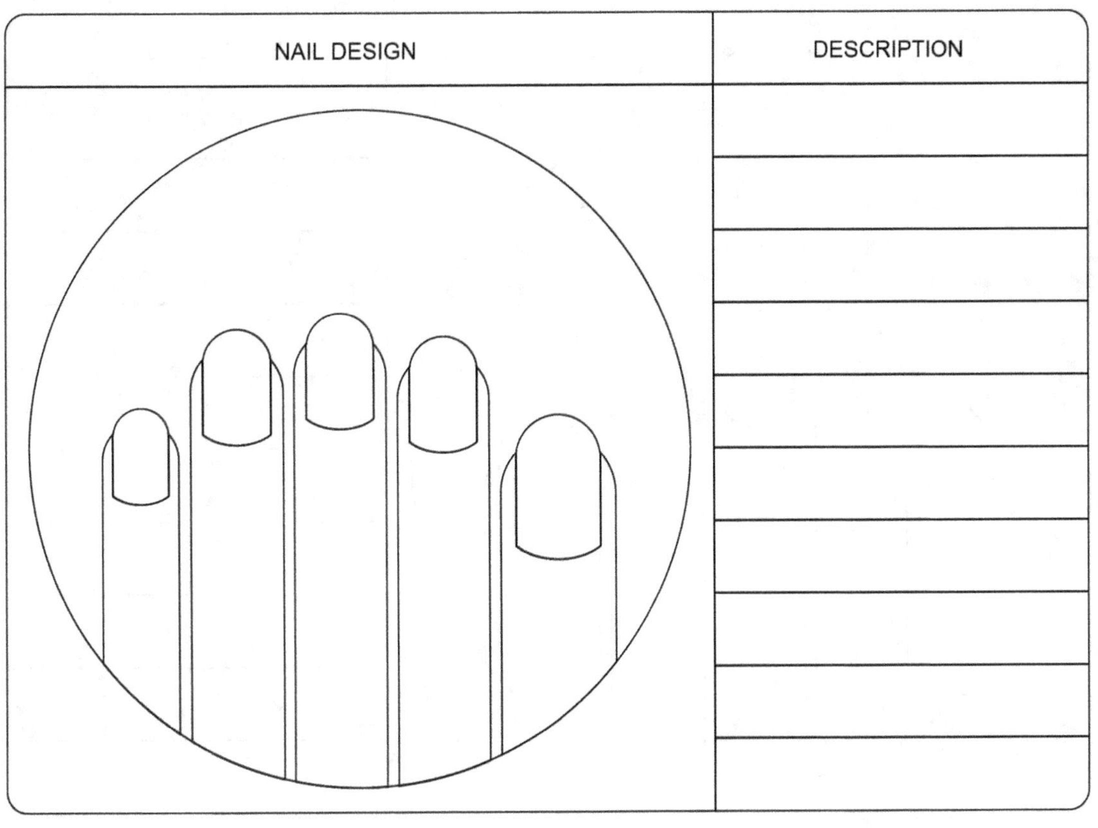	

COLOR PALETTE

1	2	3	4	5	6	7	8

NR	COLOR	BRAND
1		
2		
3		
4		
5		
6		
7		
8		

DETAILS & PATTERNS

ADDITIONAL NOTES

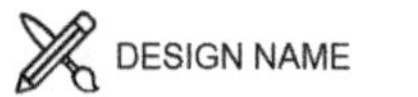
DESIGN NAME ....

DATE ....

NAIL DESIGN	DESCRIPTION

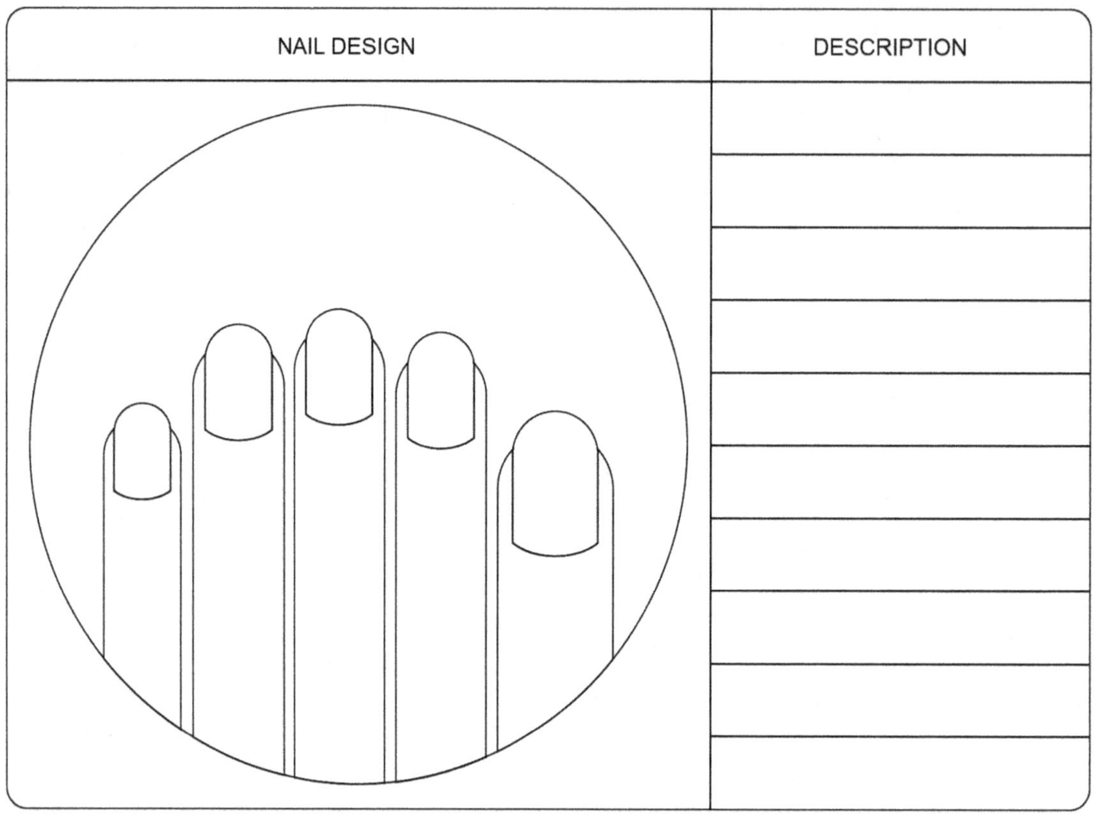

COLOR PALETTE

1	2	3	4	5	6	7	8

NR	COLOR	BRAND
1		
2		
3		
4		
5		
6		
7		
8		

DETAILS & PATTERNS

ADDITIONAL NOTES

DESIGN NAME .... DATE ....

NAIL DESIGN	DESCRIPTION

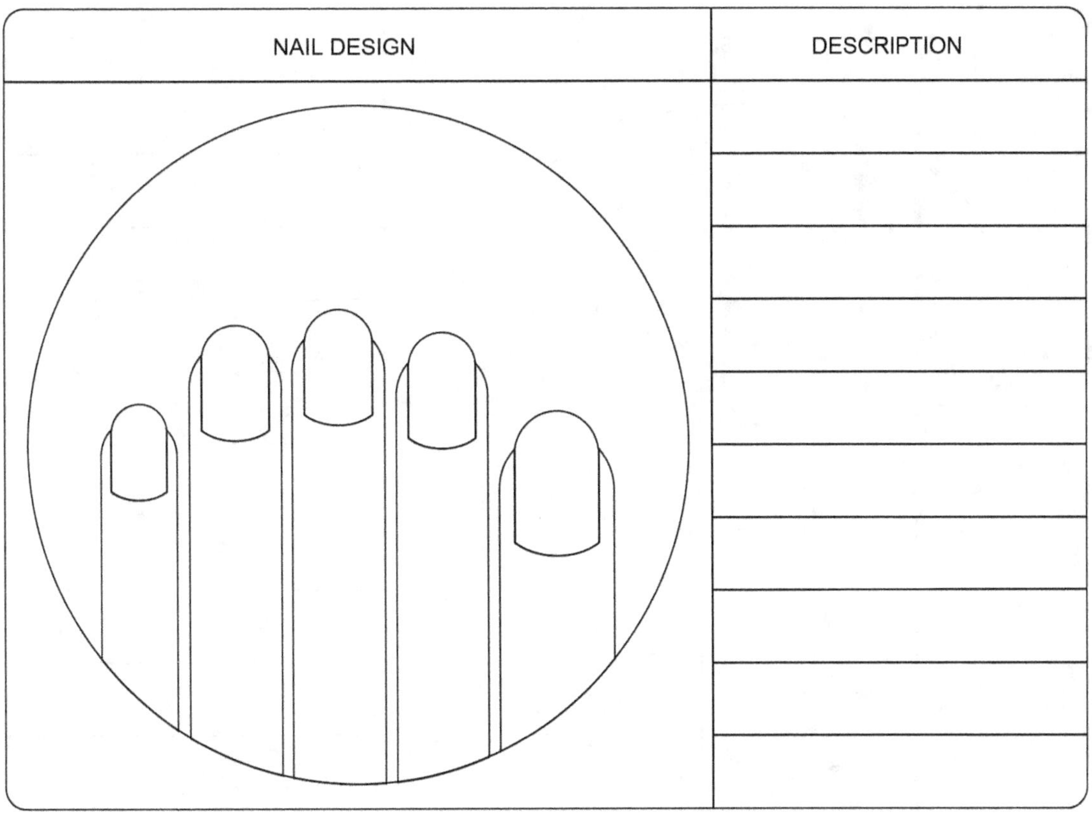

COLOR PALETTE

1	2	3	4	5	6	7	8

NR	COLOR	BRAND
1		
2		
3		
4		
5		
6		
7		
8		

DETAILS & PATTERNS

ADDITIONAL NOTES

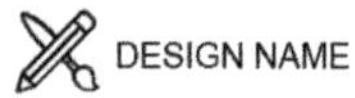 DESIGN NAME ....

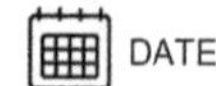 DATE ....

NAIL DESIGN	DESCRIPTION
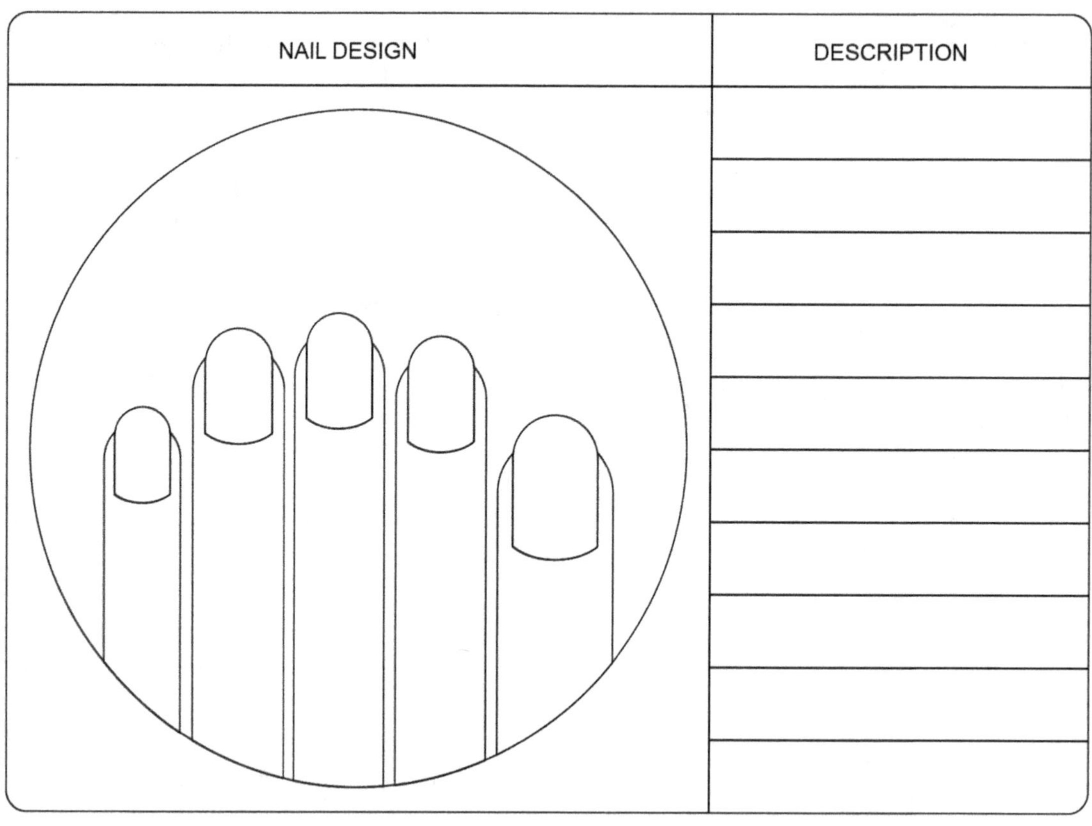	

COLOR PALETTE

1	2	3	4	5	6	7	8

NR	COLOR	BRAND
1		
2		
3		
4		
5		
6		
7		
8		

DETAILS & PATTERNS

ADDITIONAL NOTES

DESIGN NAME .... DATE ....

NAIL DESIGN	DESCRIPTION

COLOR PALETTE							
1	2	3	4	5	6	7	8

NR	COLOR	BRAND
1		
2		
3		
4		
5		
6		
7		
8		

DETAILS & PATTERNS

ADDITIONAL NOTES

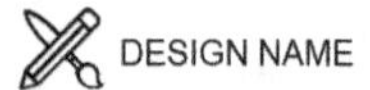

DESIGN NAME ....

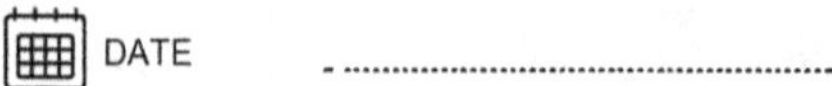

DATE ....

NAIL DESIGN	DESCRIPTION

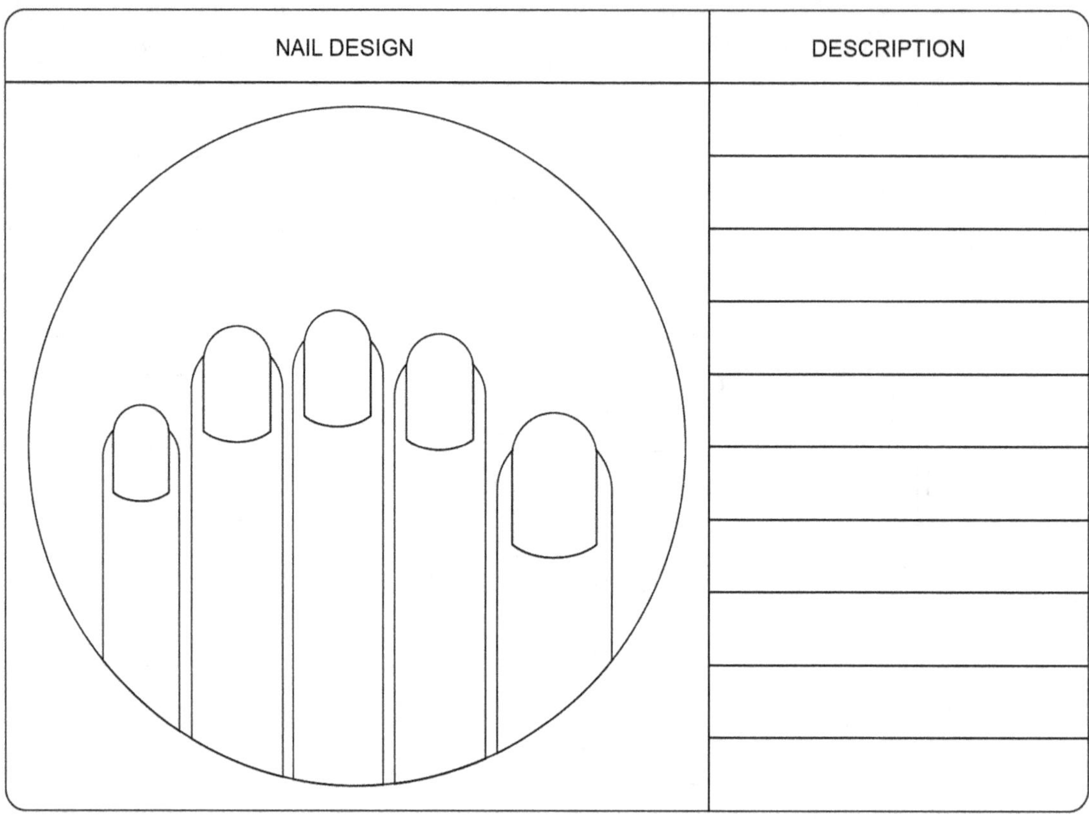

COLOR PALETTE

1	2	3	4	5	6	7	8

NR	COLOR	BRAND
1		
2		
3		
4		
5		
6		
7		
8		

DETAILS & PATTERNS

ADDITIONAL NOTES

DESIGN NAME .... DATE ....

NAIL DESIGN	DESCRIPTION

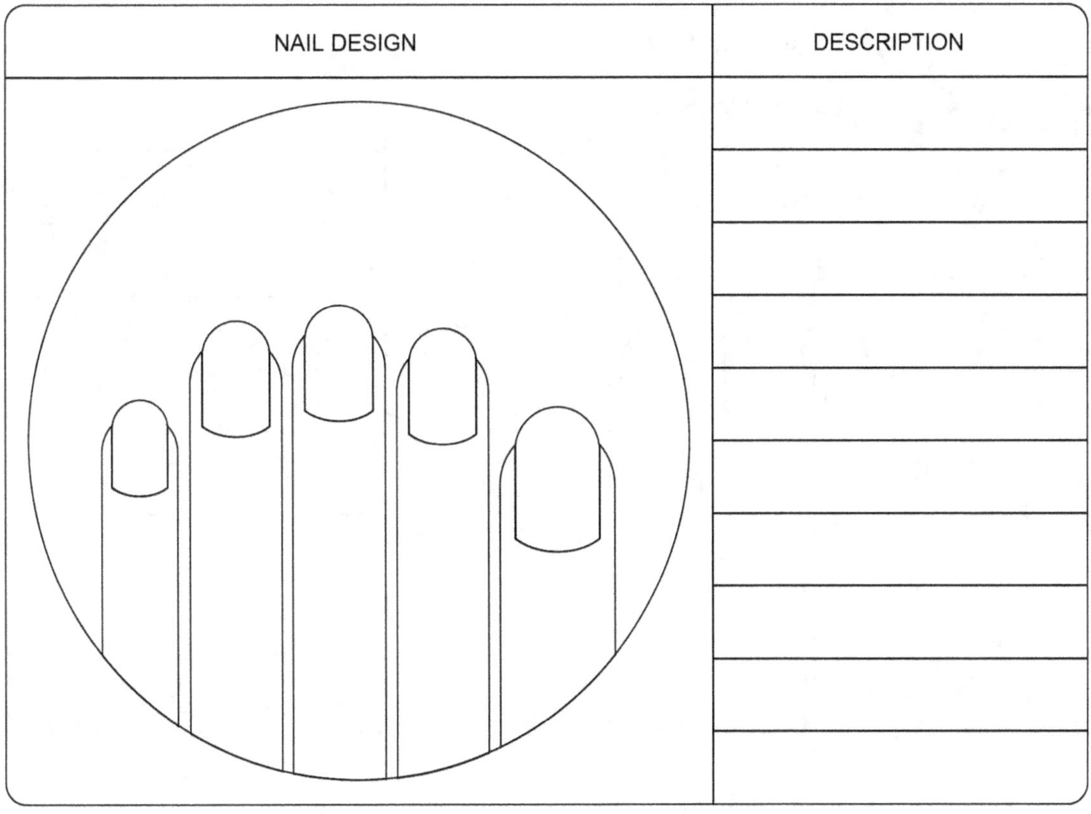

COLOR PALETTE

1	2	3	4	5	6	7	8

NR	COLOR	BRAND
1		
2		
3		
4		
5		
6		
7		
8		

DETAILS & PATTERNS

ADDITIONAL NOTES

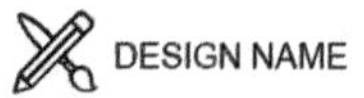
DESIGN NAME
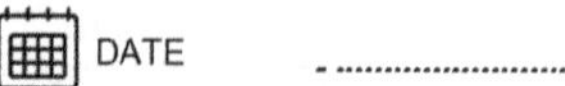
DATE

NAIL DESIGN	DESCRIPTION
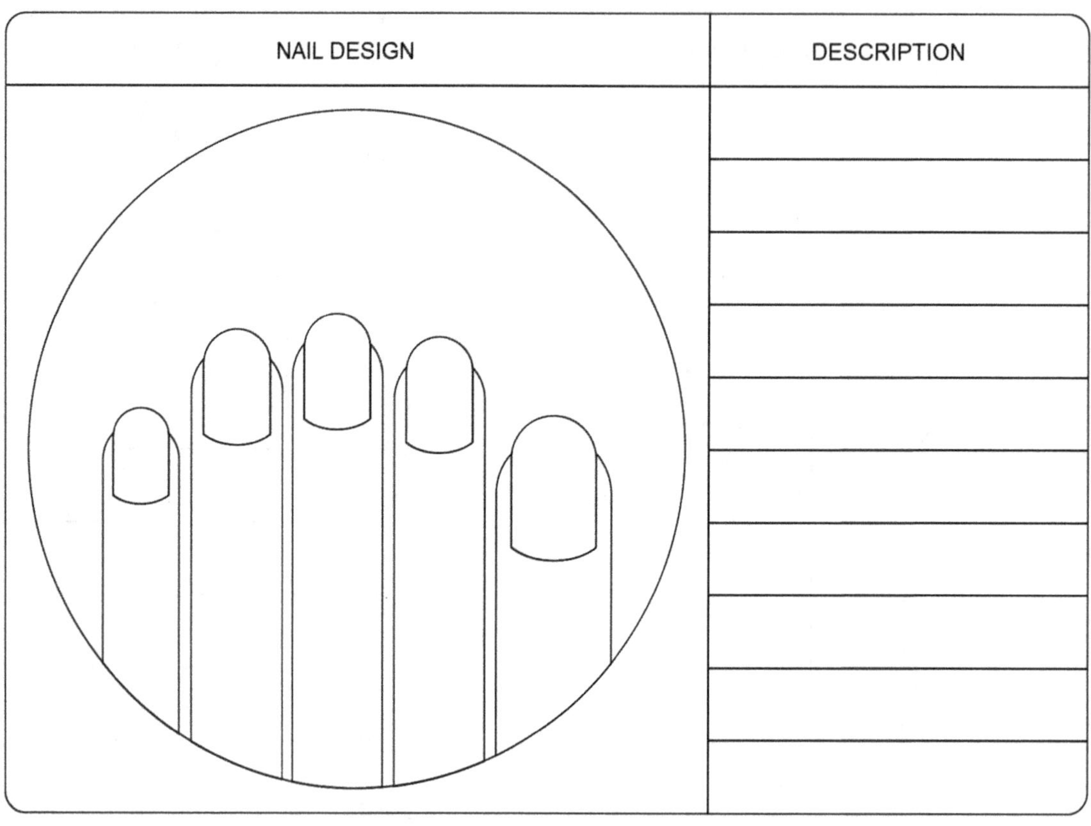	

COLOR PALETTE

1	2	3	4	5	6	7	8

NR	COLOR	BRAND
1		
2		
3		
4		
5		
6		
7		
8		

DETAILS & PATTERNS

ADDITIONAL NOTES

DESIGN NAME .... DATE ....

NAIL DESIGN	DESCRIPTION
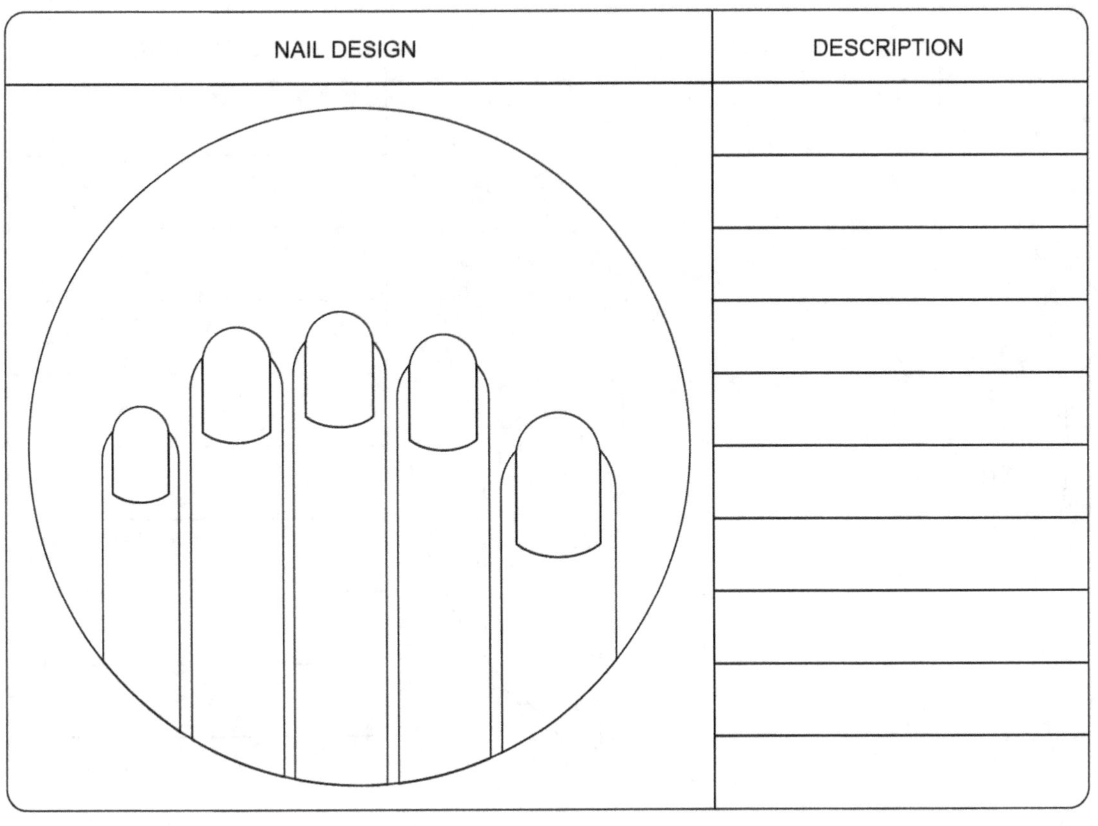	

COLOR PALETTE

1	2	3	4	5	6	7	8

NR	COLOR	BRAND
1		
2		
3		
4		
5		
6		
7		
8		

DETAILS & PATTERNS

ADDITIONAL NOTES

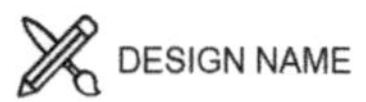 DESIGN NAME ....

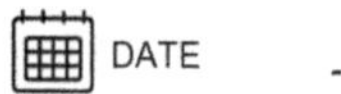 DATE ....

NAIL DESIGN	DESCRIPTION
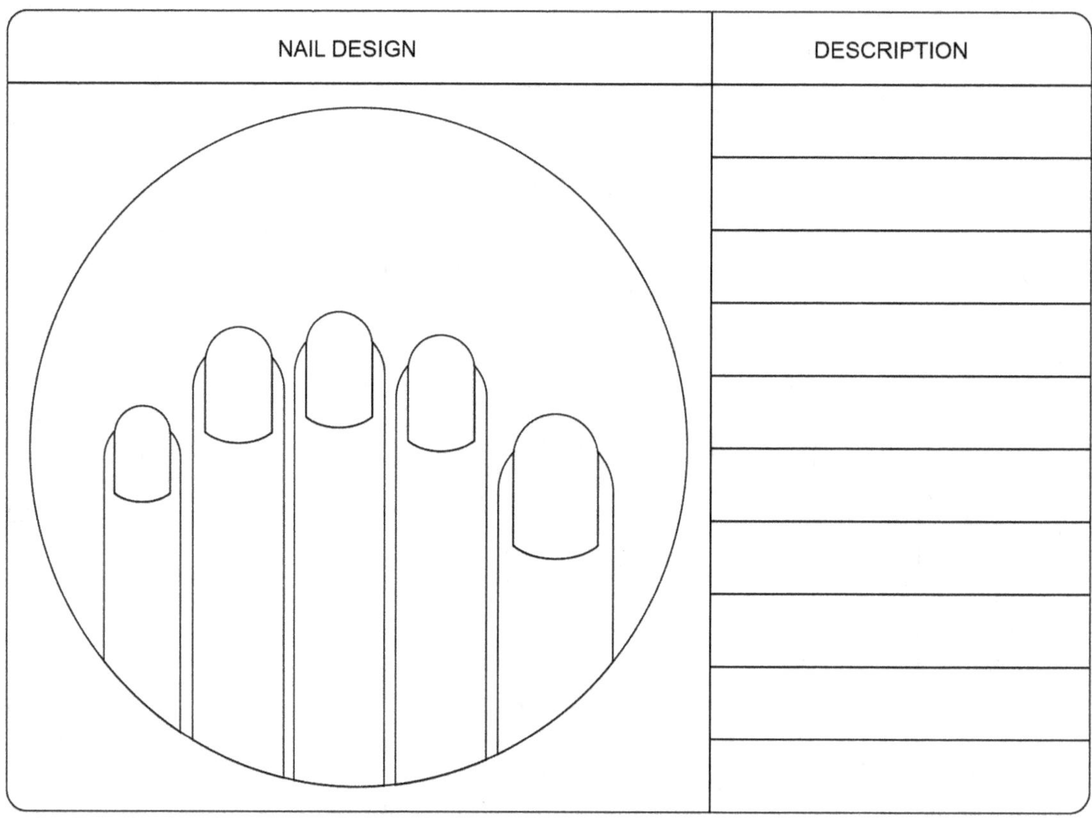	

COLOR PALETTE

1	2	3	4	5	6	7	8

NR	COLOR	BRAND
1		
2		
3		
4		
5		
6		
7		
8		

DETAILS & PATTERNS

ADDITIONAL NOTES

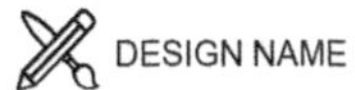 DESIGN NAME ....

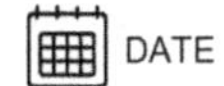 DATE ....

NAIL DESIGN	DESCRIPTION
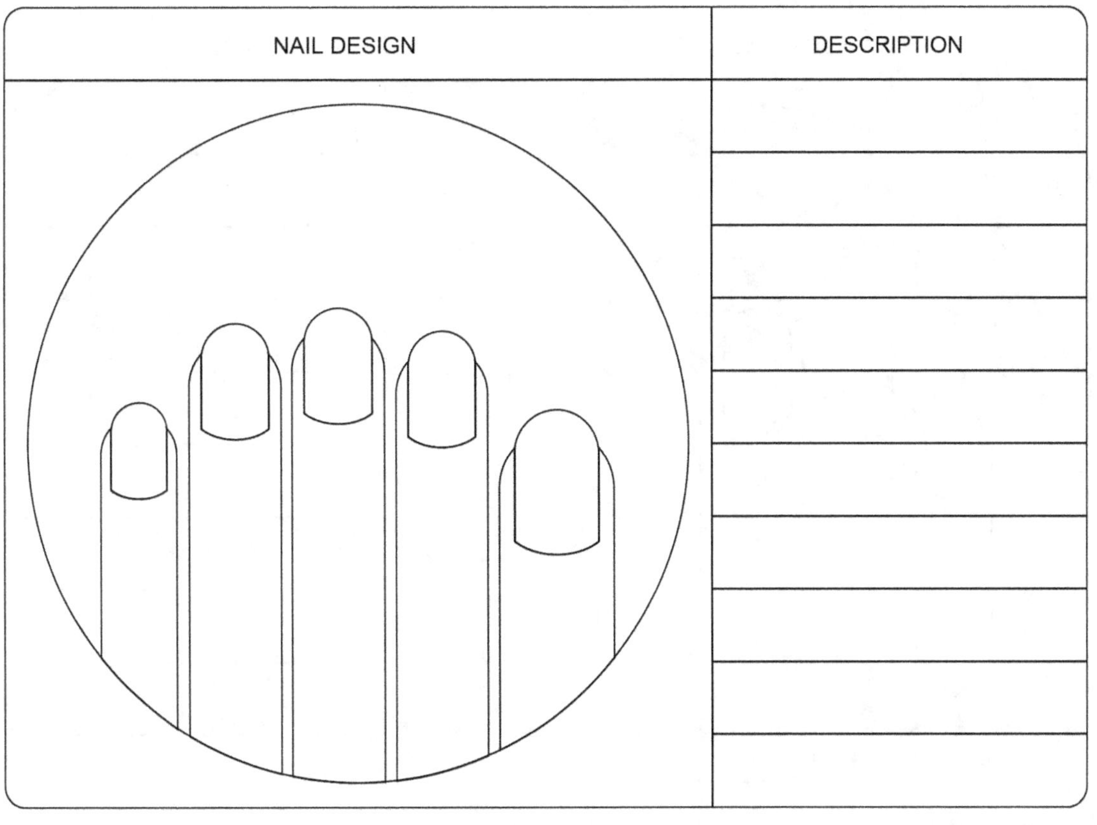	

COLOR PALETTE							
1	2	3	4	5	6	7	8

NR	COLOR	BRAND
1		
2		
3		
4		
5		
6		
7		
8		

DETAILS & PATTERNS

ADDITIONAL NOTES

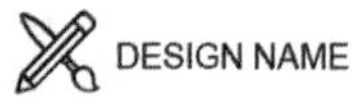 DESIGN NAME ....

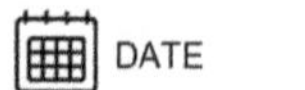 DATE ....

NAIL DESIGN	DESCRIPTION
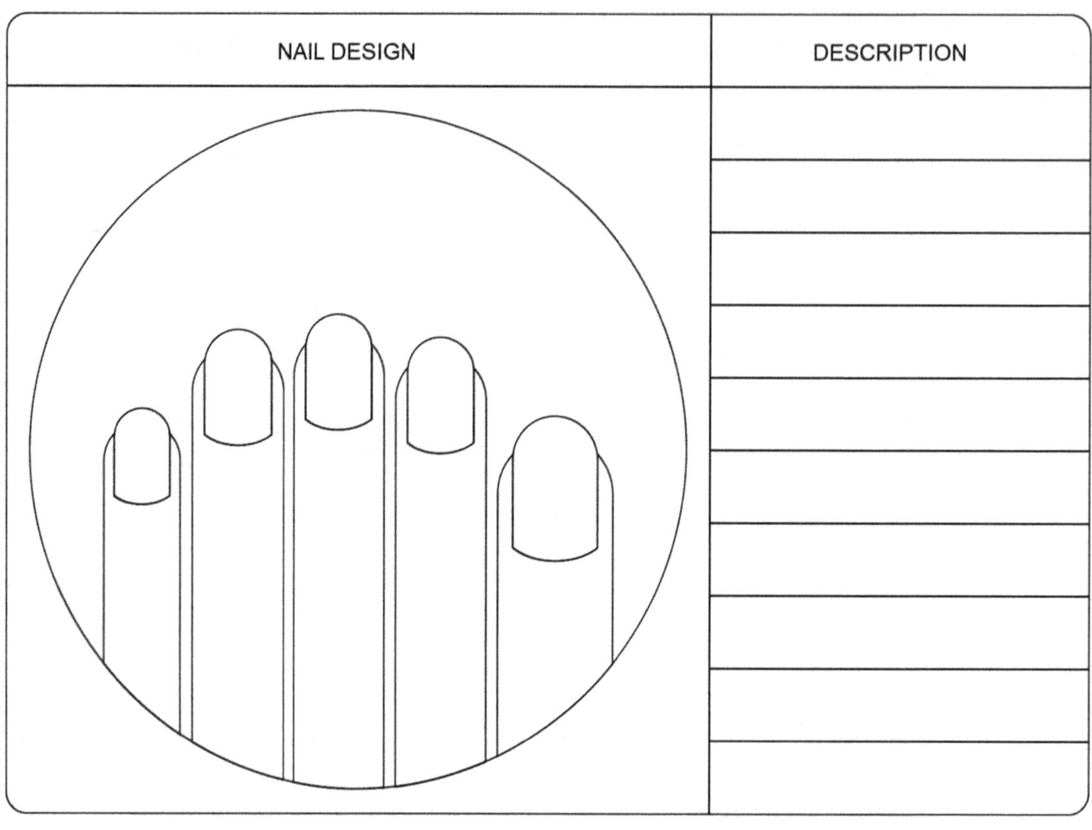	

COLOR PALETTE							
1	2	3	4	5	6	7	8

NR	COLOR	BRAND
1		
2		
3		
4		
5		
6		
7		
8		

DETAILS & PATTERNS

ADDITIONAL NOTES

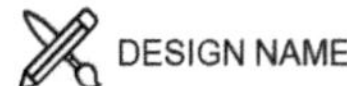 DESIGN NAME ....

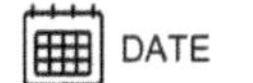 DATE ....

NAIL DESIGN	DESCRIPTION
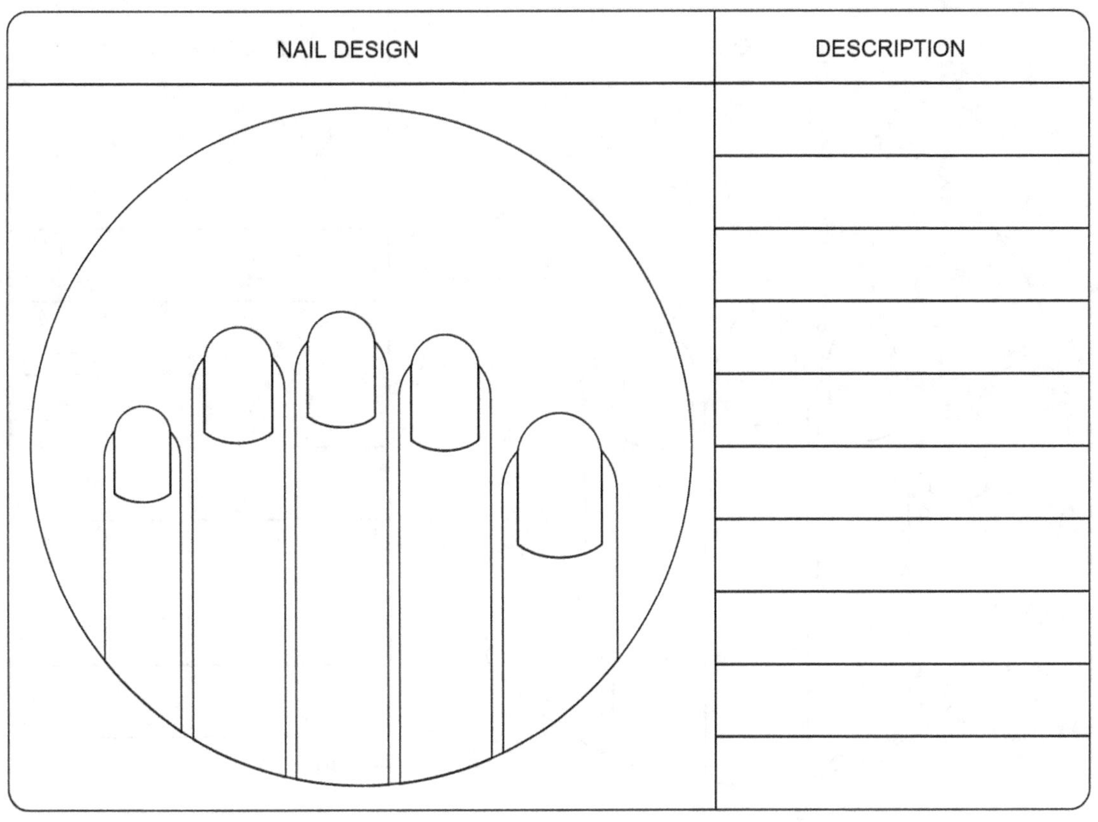	

COLOR PALETTE

1	2	3	4	5	6	7	8

NR	COLOR	BRAND
1		
2		
3		
4		
5		
6		
7		
8		

DETAILS & PATTERNS

ADDITIONAL NOTES

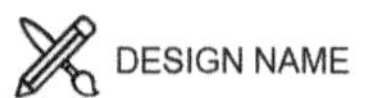

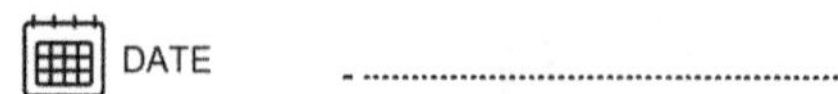

NAIL DESIGN	DESCRIPTION

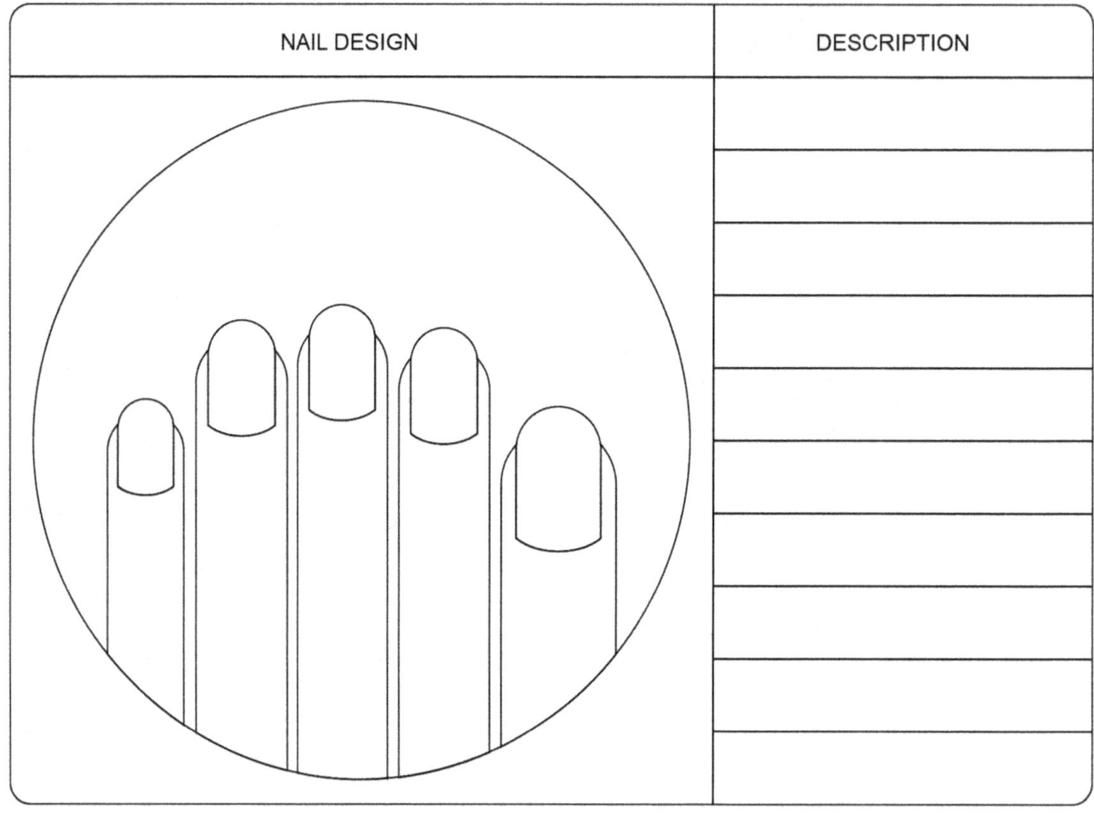

COLOR PALETTE							
1	2	3	4	5	6	7	8

NR	COLOR	BRAND
1		
2		
3		
4		
5		
6		
7		
8		

DETAILS & PATTERNS

ADDITIONAL NOTES

DESIGN NAME .... DATE ....

NAIL DESIGN	DESCRIPTION
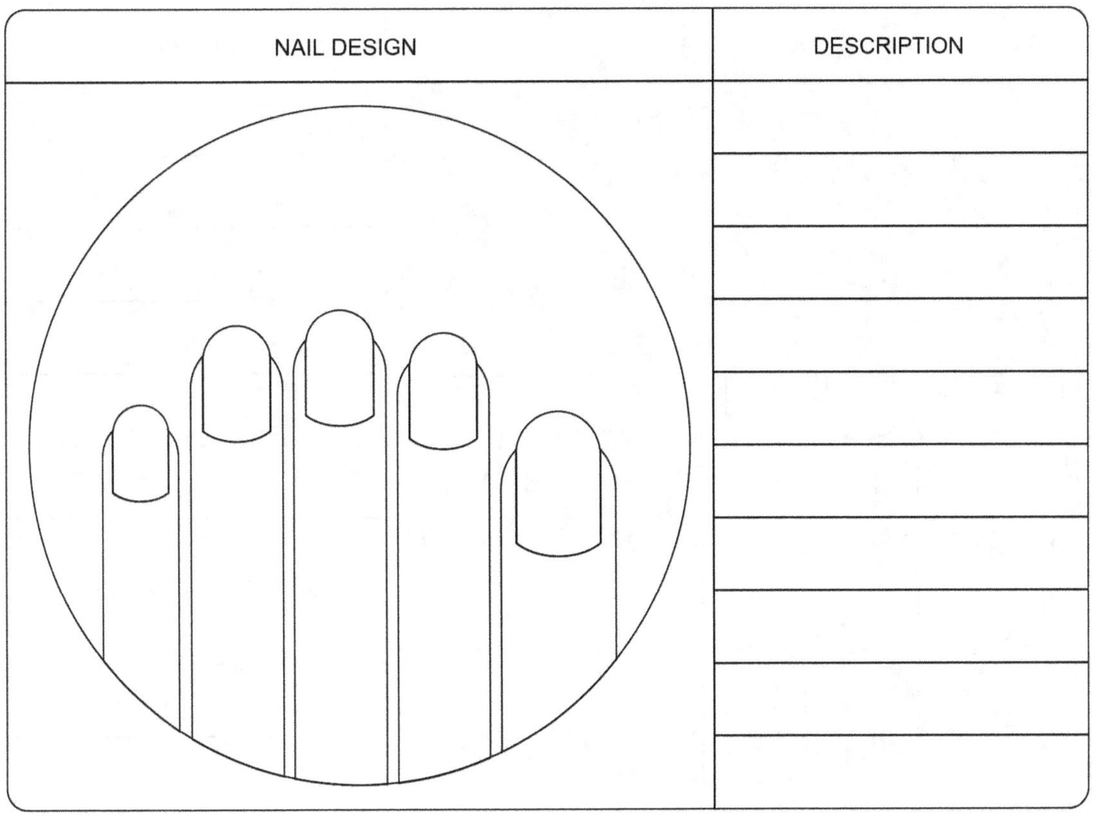	

COLOR PALETTE

1	2	3	4	5	6	7	8

NR	COLOR	BRAND
1		
2		
3		
4		
5		
6		
7		
8		

DETAILS & PATTERNS

ADDITIONAL NOTES

DESIGN NAME .... DATE ....

NAIL DESIGN	DESCRIPTION
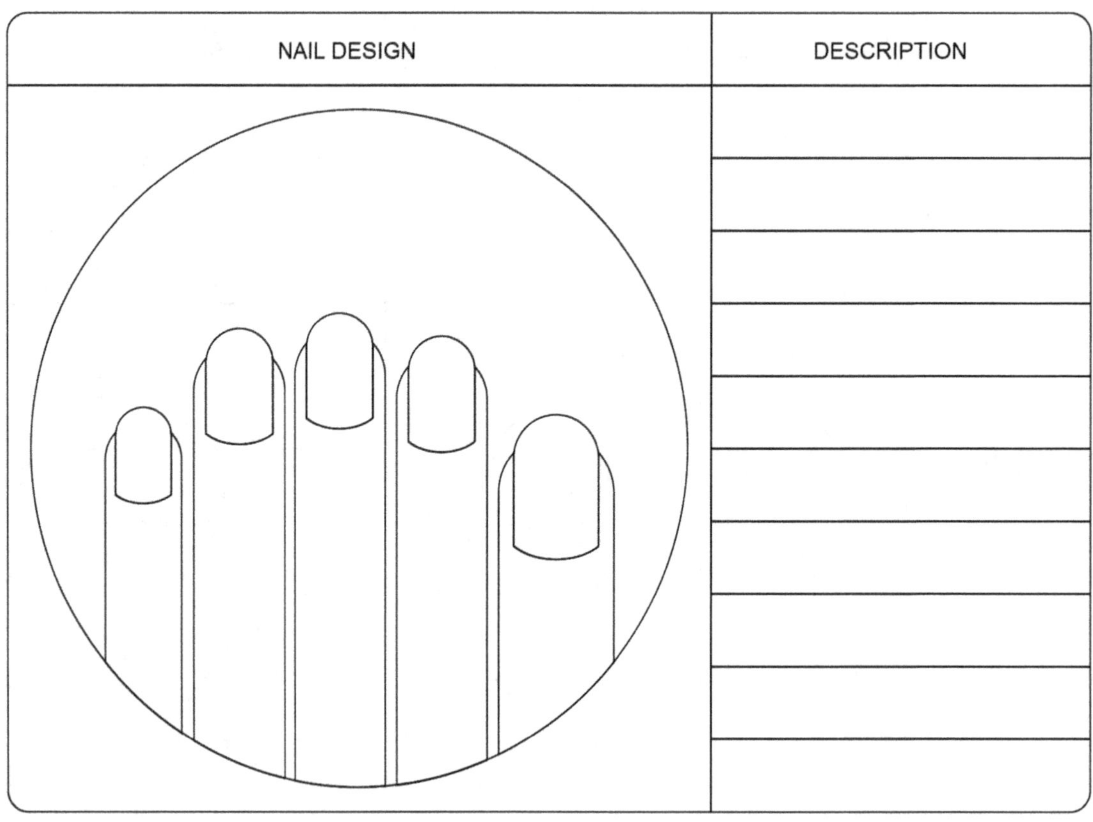	

COLOR PALETTE

1	2	3	4	5	6	7	8

NR	COLOR	BRAND
1		
2		
3		
4		
5		
6		
7		
8		

DETAILS & PATTERNS

ADDITIONAL NOTES

DESIGN NAME .... DATE ....

NAIL DESIGN	DESCRIPTION
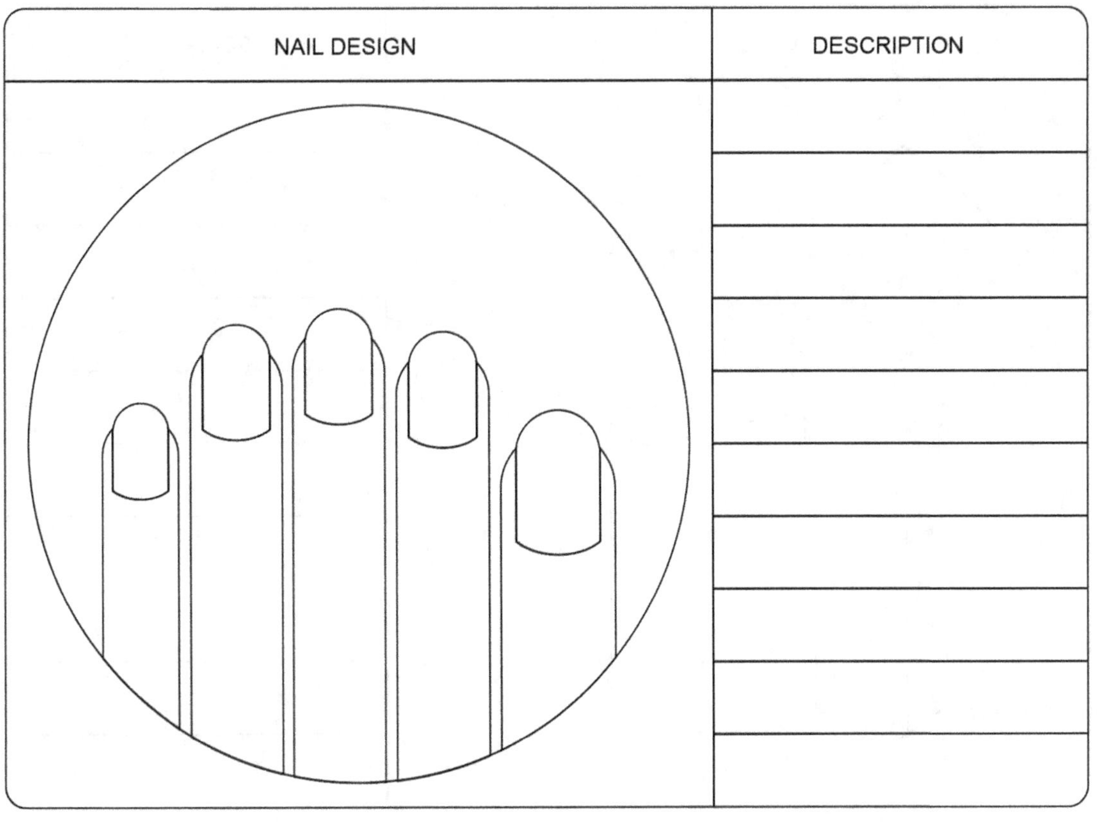	

COLOR PALETTE

1	2	3	4	5	6	7	8

NR	COLOR	BRAND
1		
2		
3		
4		
5		
6		
7		
8		

DETAILS & PATTERNS

ADDITIONAL NOTES

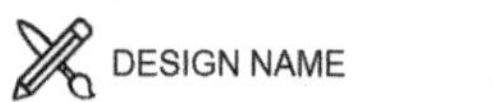

DESIGN NAME .... DATE ....

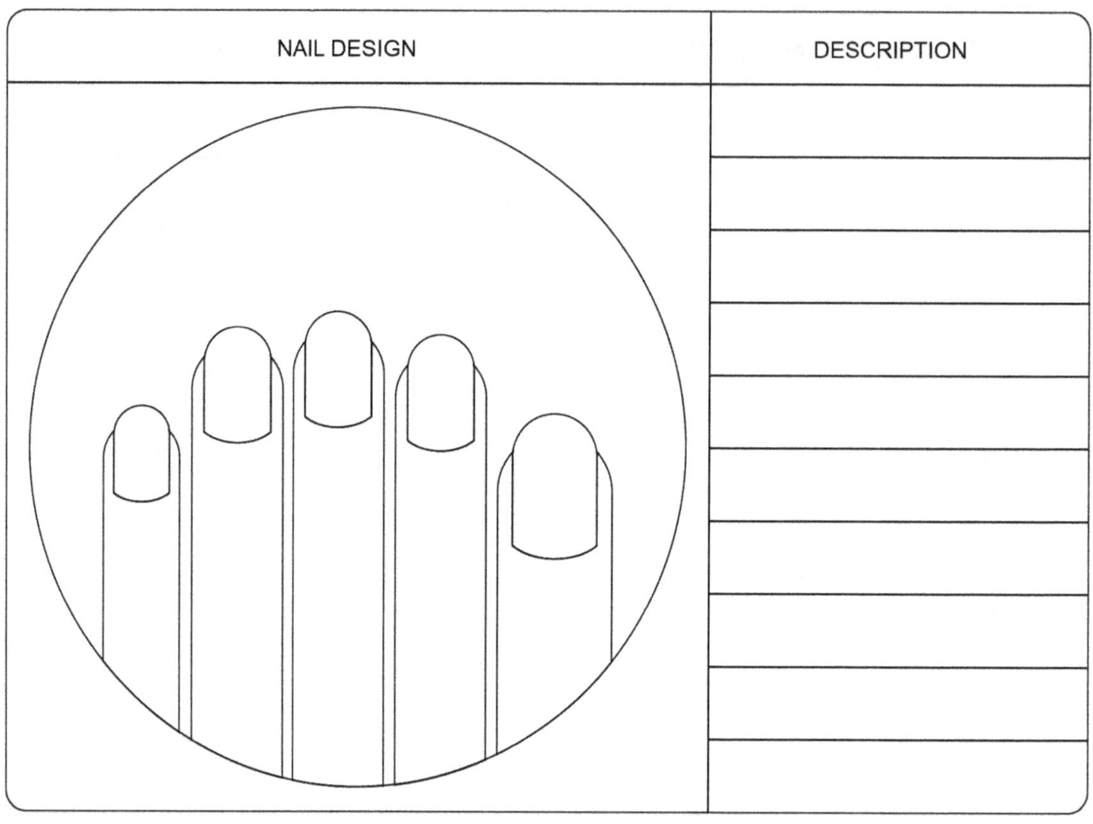

COLOR PALETTE

1	2	3	4	5	6	7	8

NR	COLOR	BRAND
1		
2		
3		
4		
5		
6		
7		
8		

DETAILS & PATTERNS

ADDITIONAL NOTES

DESIGN NAME .... DATE ....

NAIL DESIGN	DESCRIPTION
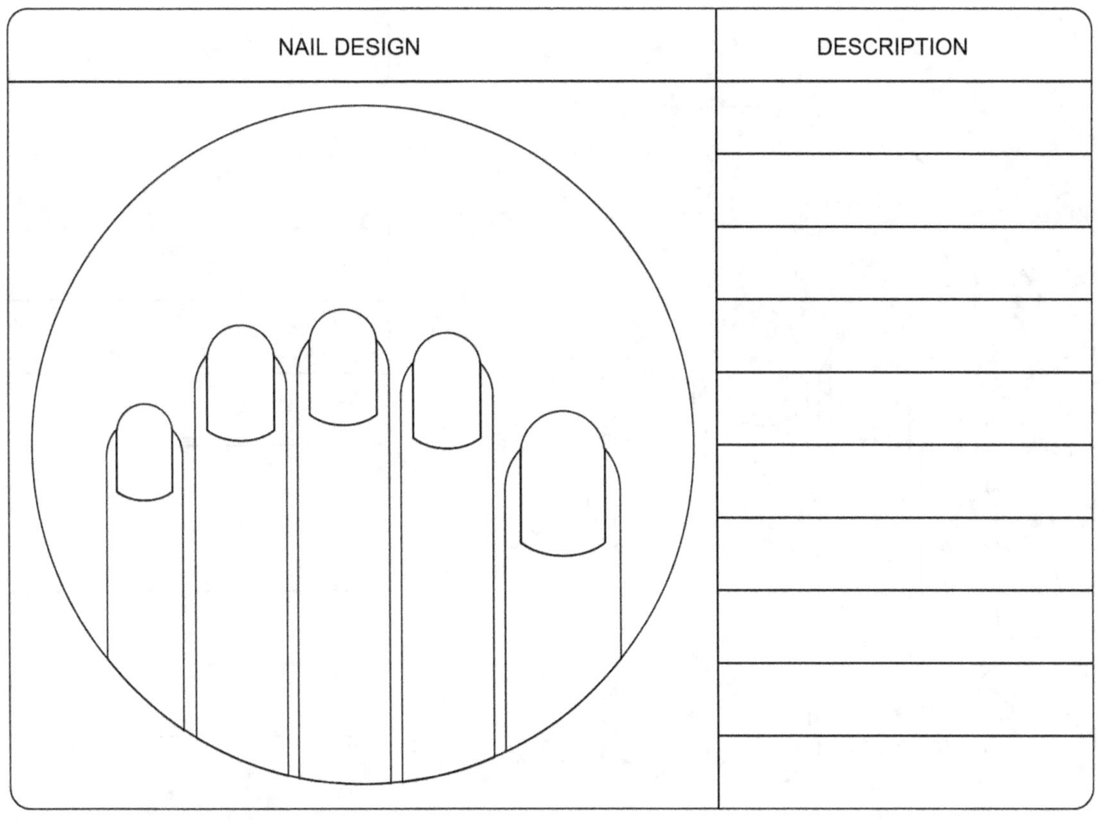	

COLOR PALETTE

1	2	3	4	5	6	7	8

NR	COLOR	BRAND
1		
2		
3		
4		
5		
6		
7		
8		

DETAILS & PATTERNS

ADDITIONAL NOTES

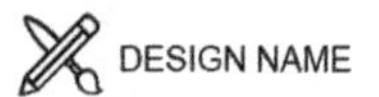
DESIGN NAME

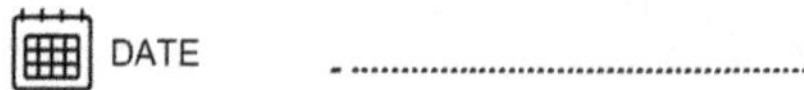
DATE

NAIL DESIGN	DESCRIPTION
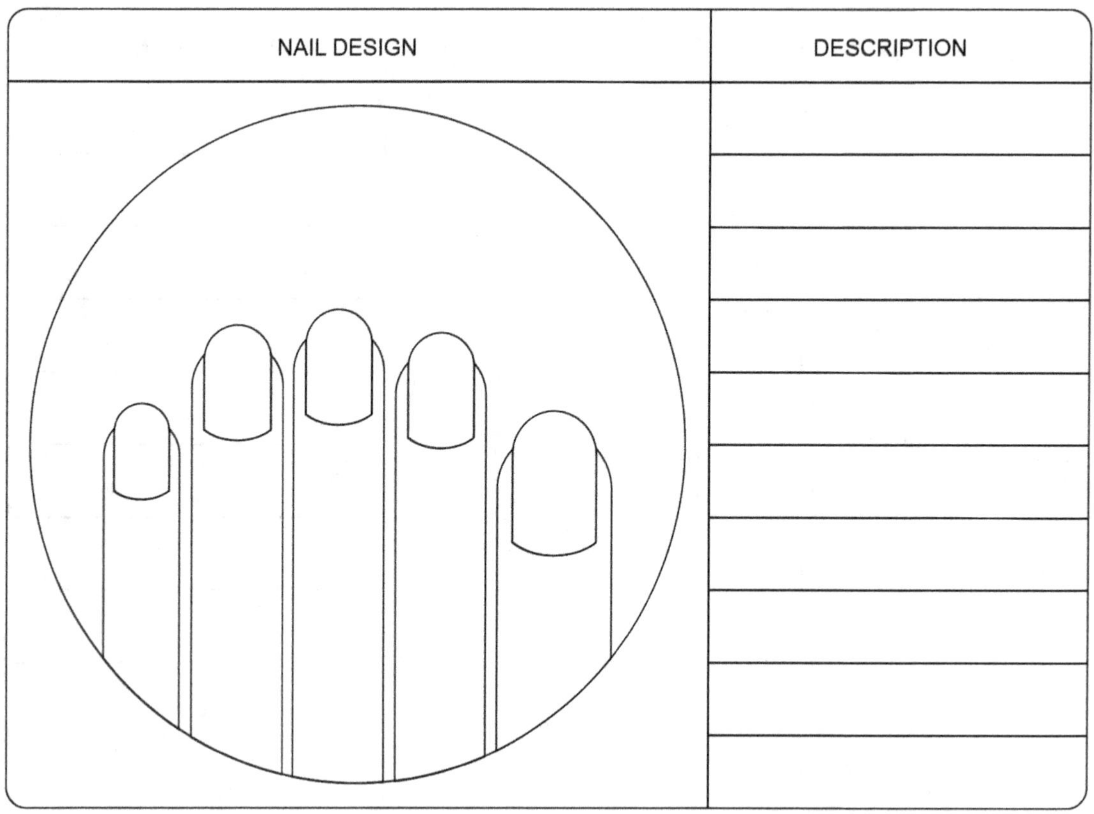	

COLOR PALETTE							
1	2	3	4	5	6	7	8

NR	COLOR	BRAND
1		
2		
3		
4		
5		
6		
7		
8		

DETAILS & PATTERNS

ADDITIONAL NOTES

DESIGN NAME .... DATE ....

NAIL DESIGN	DESCRIPTION
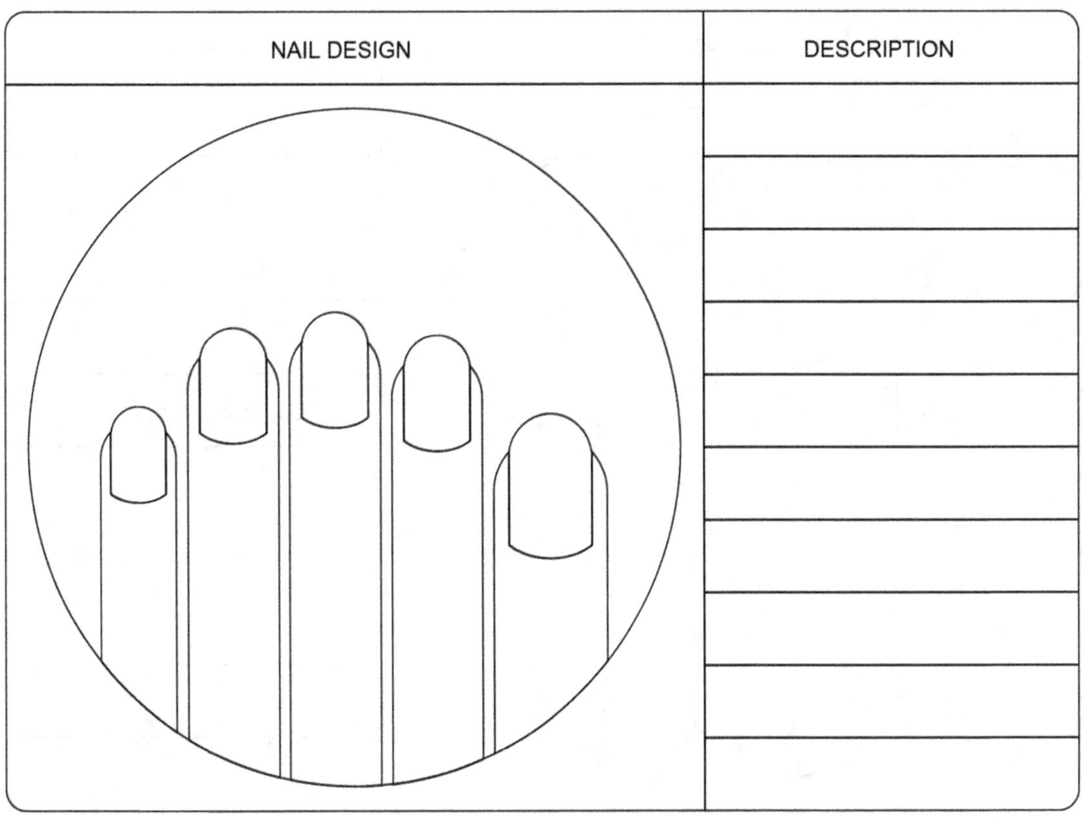	

COLOR PALETTE

1	2	3	4	5	6	7	8

NR	COLOR	BRAND
1		
2		
3		
4		
5		
6		
7		
8		

DETAILS & PATTERNS

ADDITIONAL NOTES

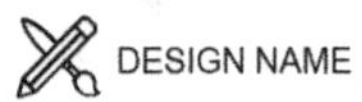 DESIGN NAME ....

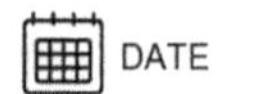 DATE ....

NAIL DESIGN	DESCRIPTION
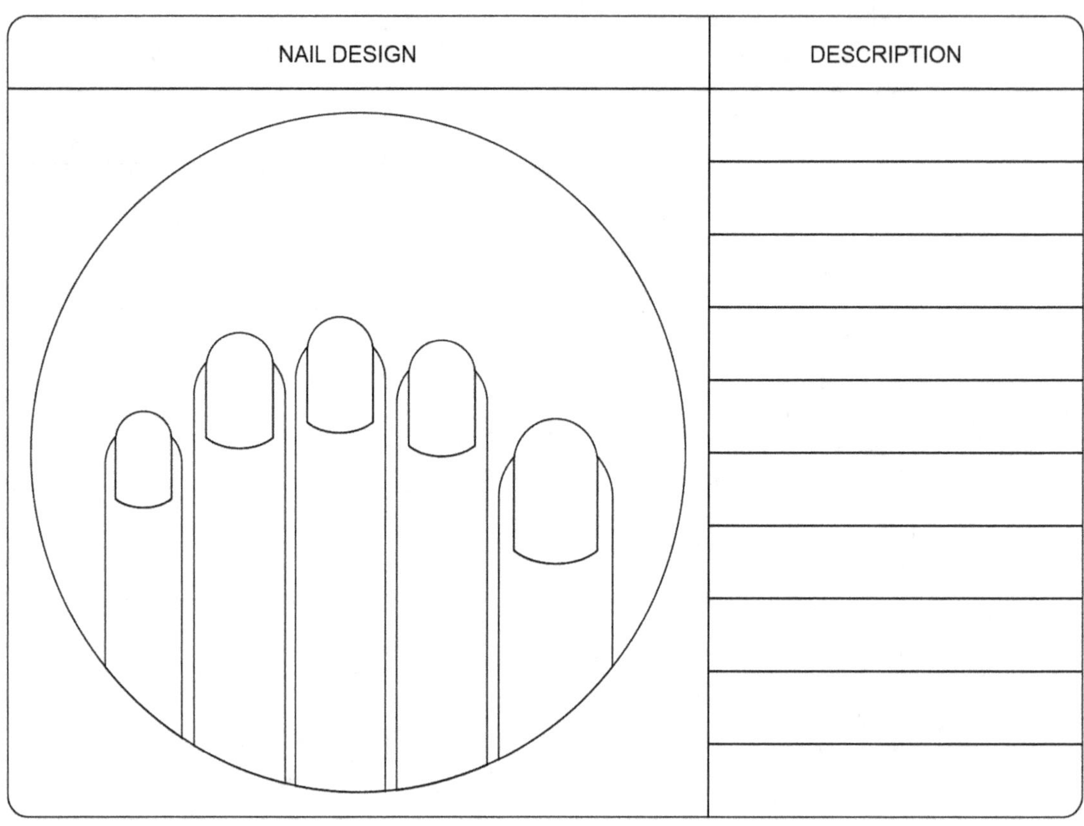	

COLOR PALETTE							
1	2	3	4	5	6	7	8

NR	COLOR	BRAND
1		
2		
3		
4		
5		
6		
7		
8		

DETAILS & PATTERNS

ADDITIONAL NOTES

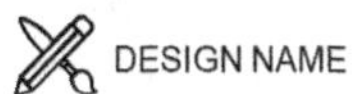
DESIGN NAME .... DATE ....

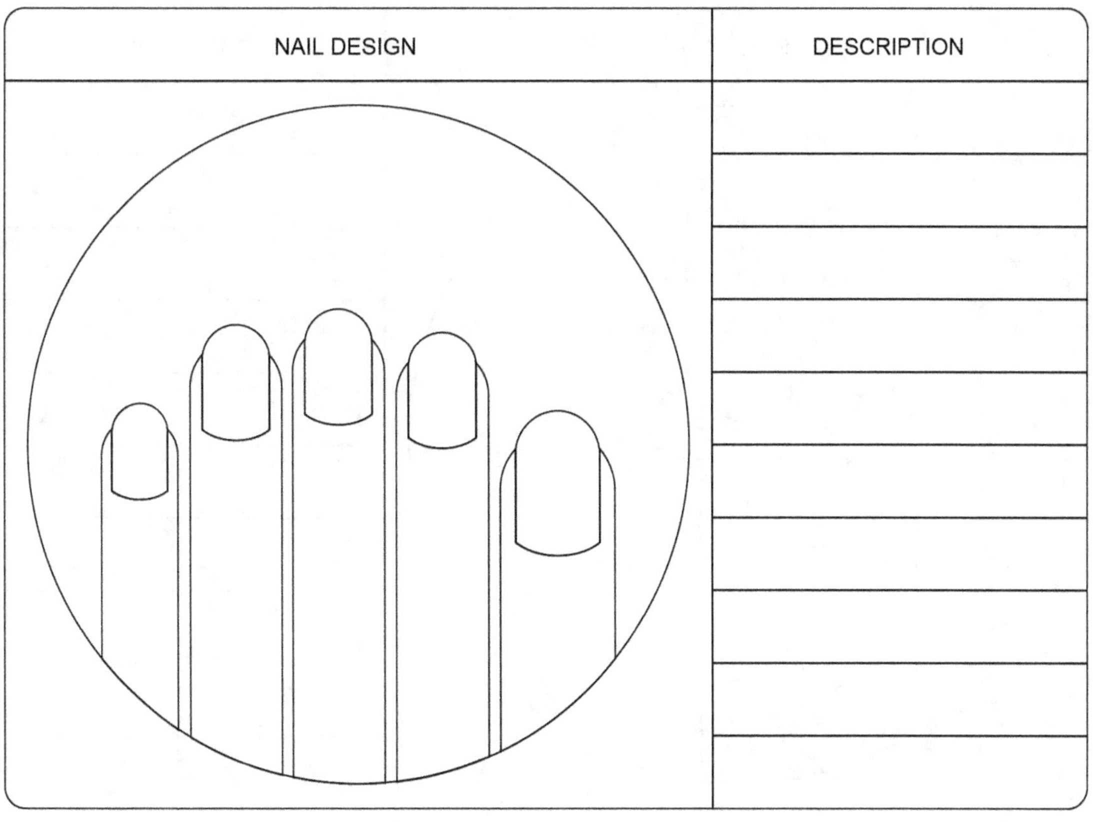

NAIL DESIGN	DESCRIPTION

COLOR PALETTE

1	2	3	4	5	6	7	8

NR	COLOR	BRAND
1		
2		
3		
4		
5		
6		
7		
8		

DETAILS & PATTERNS

ADDITIONAL NOTES

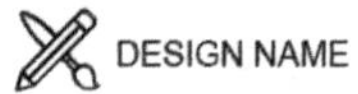
DESIGN NAME ....

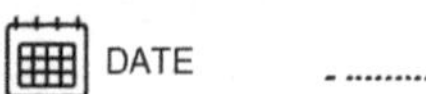
DATE ....

NAIL DESIGN	DESCRIPTION
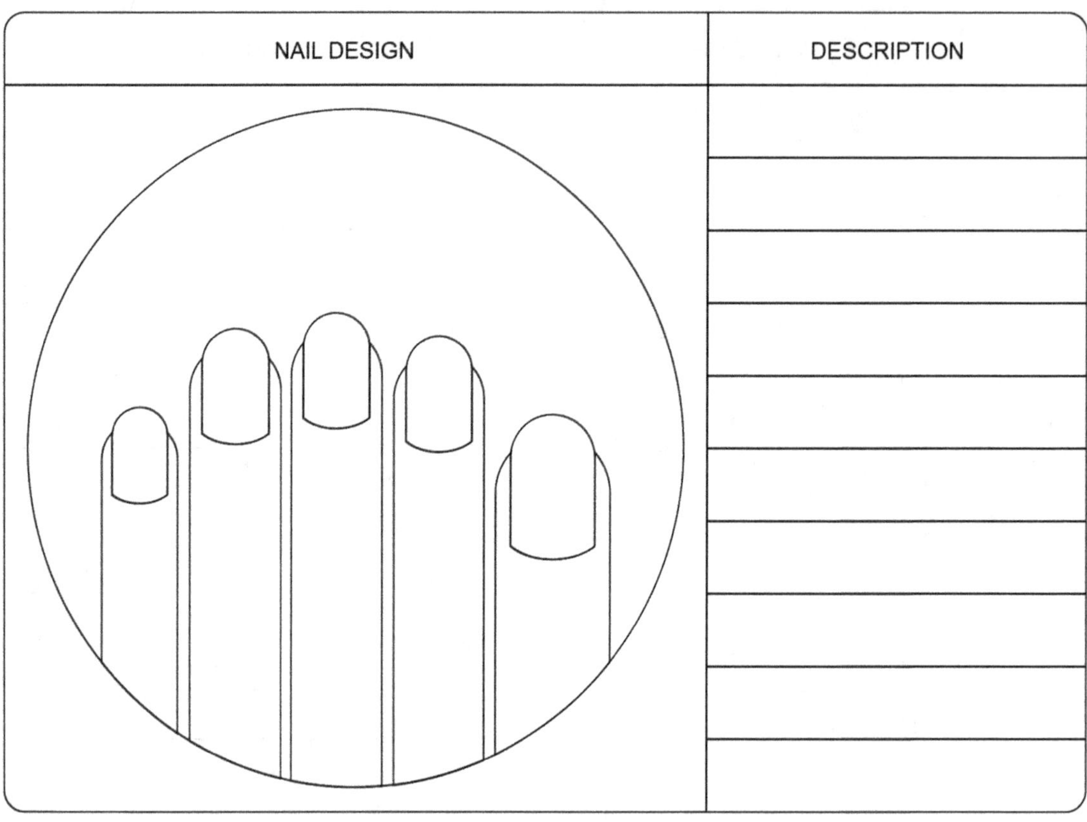	

COLOR PALETTE

1	2	3	4	5	6	7	8

NR	COLOR	BRAND
1		
2		
3		
4		
5		
6		
7		
8		

DETAILS & PATTERNS

ADDITIONAL NOTES

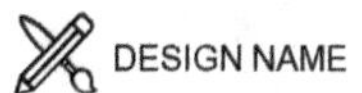 DESIGN NAME ....

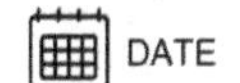 DATE ....

NAIL DESIGN	DESCRIPTION
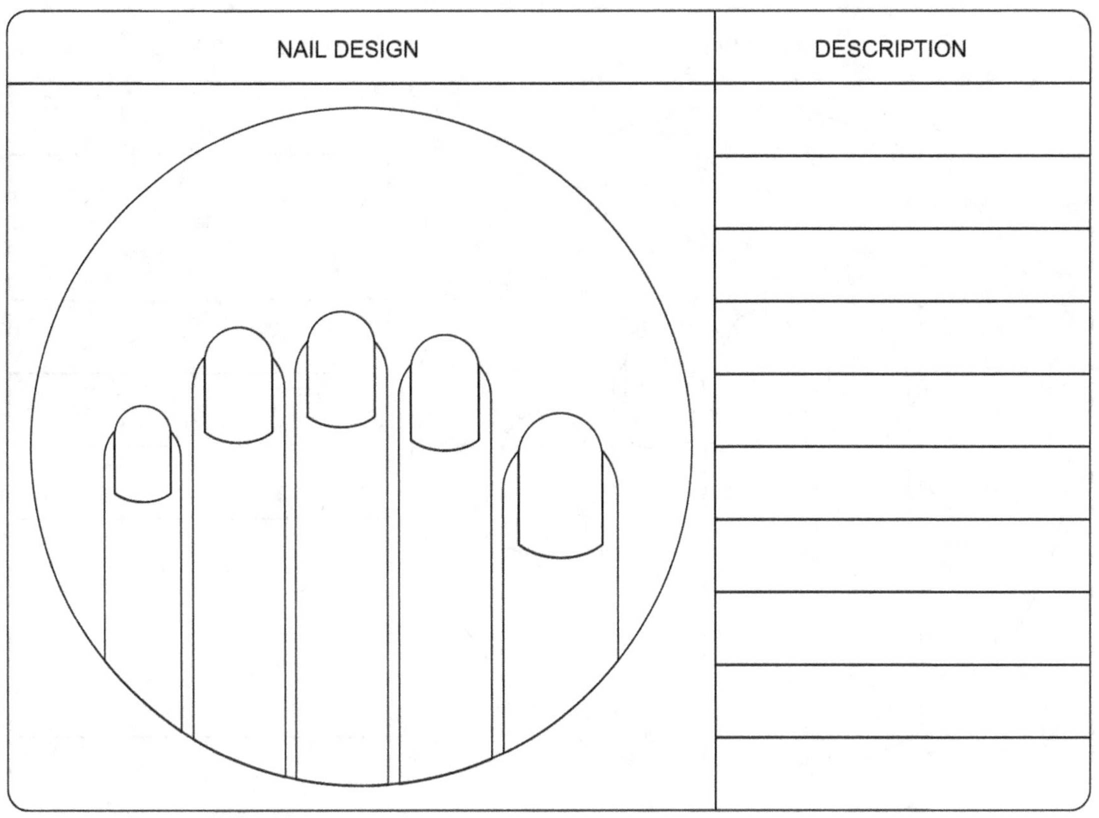	

COLOR PALETTE

1	2	3	4	5	6	7	8

NR	COLOR	BRAND
1		
2		
3		
4		
5		
6		
7		
8		

DETAILS & PATTERNS

ADDITIONAL NOTES

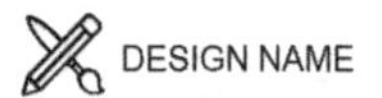

DESIGN NAME ....

DATE ....

NAIL DESIGN	DESCRIPTION
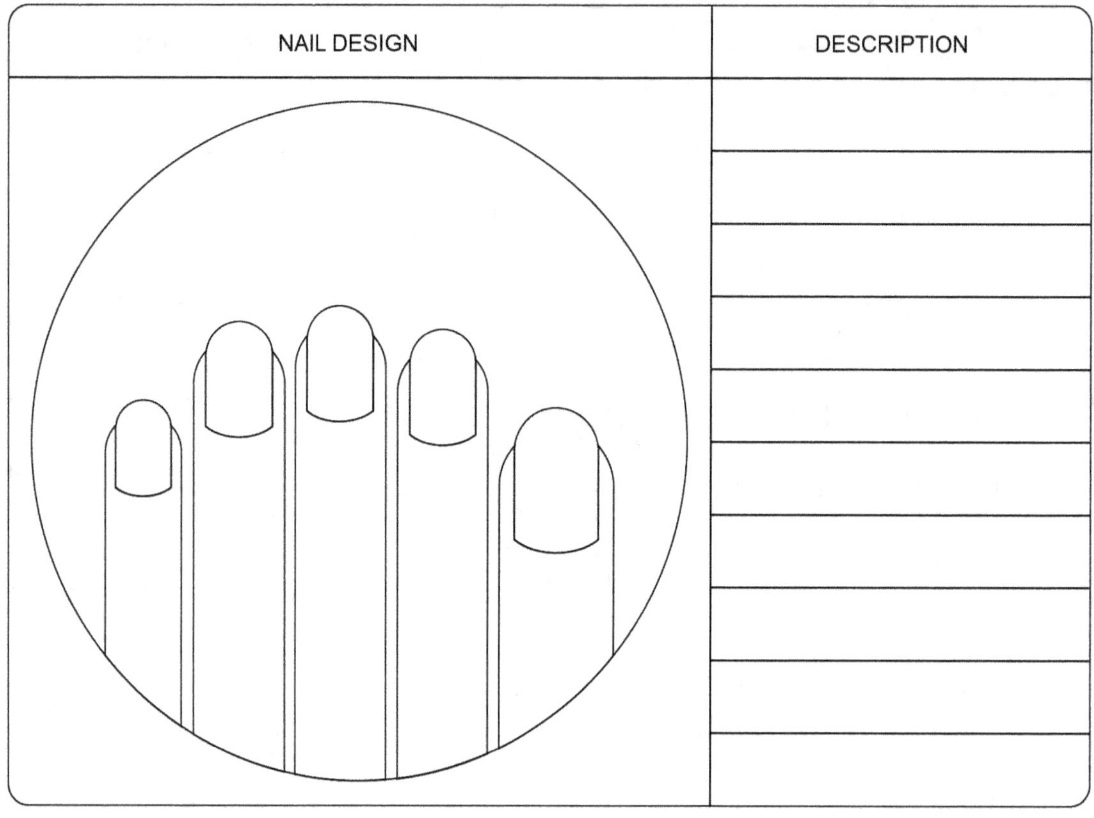	

COLOR PALETTE

1	2	3	4	5	6	7	8

NR	COLOR	BRAND
1		
2		
3		
4		
5		
6		
7		
8		

DETAILS & PATTERNS

ADDITIONAL NOTES

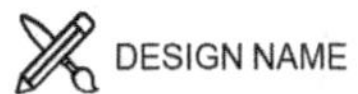

DATE ....

NAIL DESIGN	DESCRIPTION
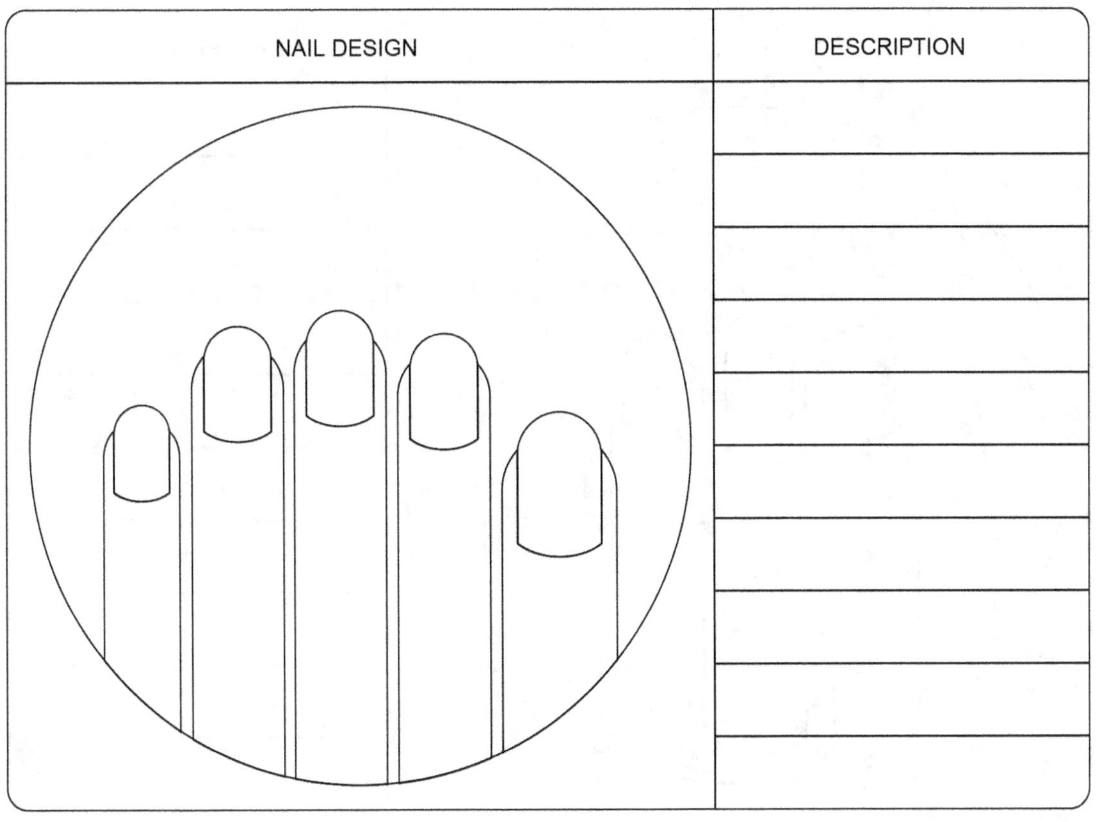	

COLOR PALETTE

1	2	3	4	5	6	7	8

NR	COLOR	BRAND
1		
2		
3		
4		
5		
6		
7		
8		

DETAILS & PATTERNS

ADDITIONAL NOTES

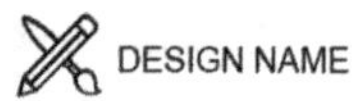
DESIGN NAME ....

DATE ....

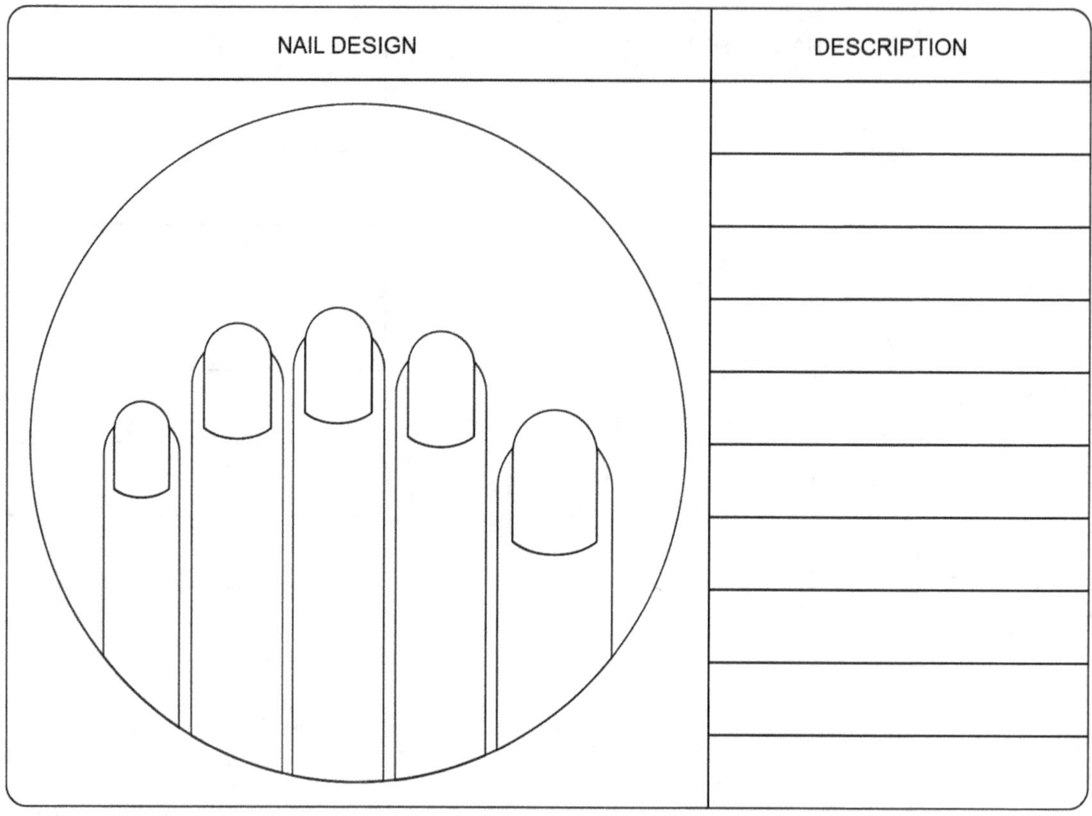

DESCRIPTION

COLOR PALETTE

1	2	3	4	5	6	7	8

NR	COLOR	BRAND
1		
2		
3		
4		
5		
6		
7		
8		

DETAILS & PATTERNS

ADDITIONAL NOTES

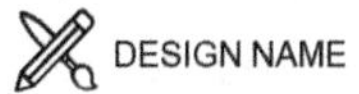 DESIGN NAME ....

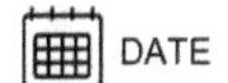 DATE ....

NAIL DESIGN	DESCRIPTION

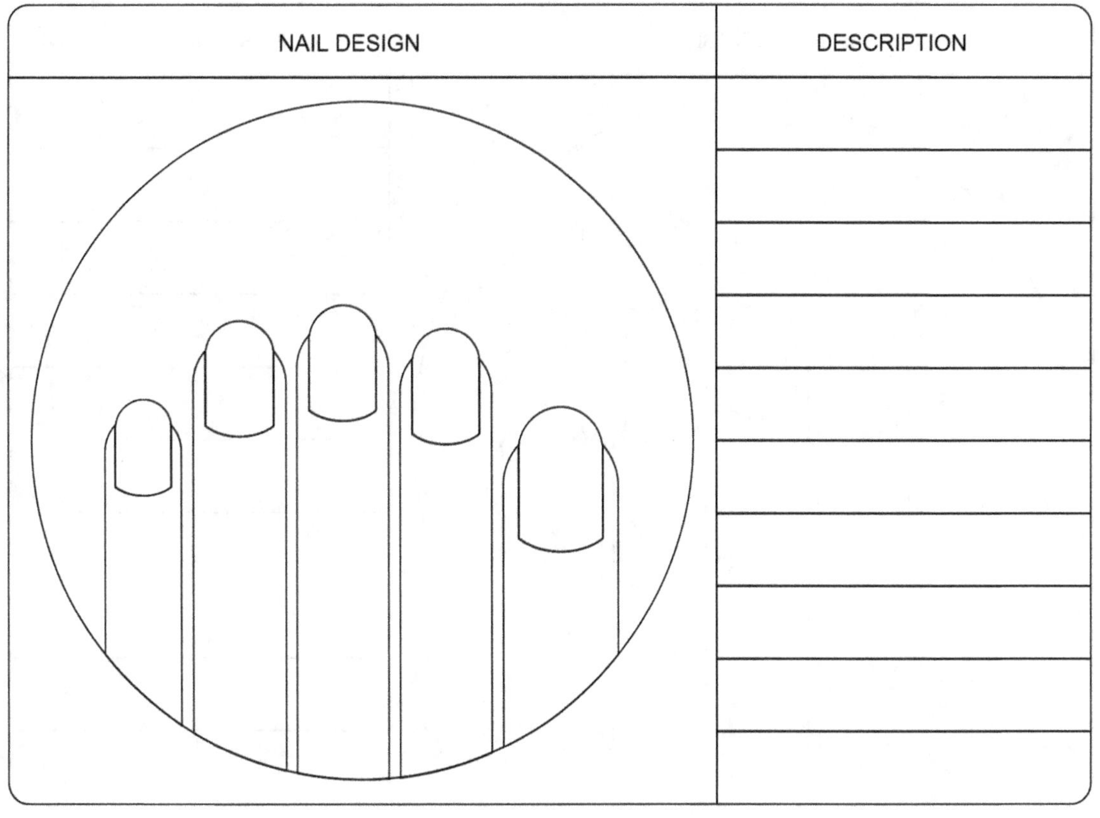

COLOR PALETTE

1	2	3	4	5	6	7	8

NR	COLOR	BRAND
1		
2		
3		
4		
5		
6		
7		
8		

DETAILS & PATTERNS

ADDITIONAL NOTES

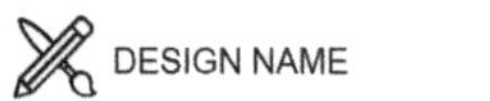

DESIGN NAME .... DATE ....

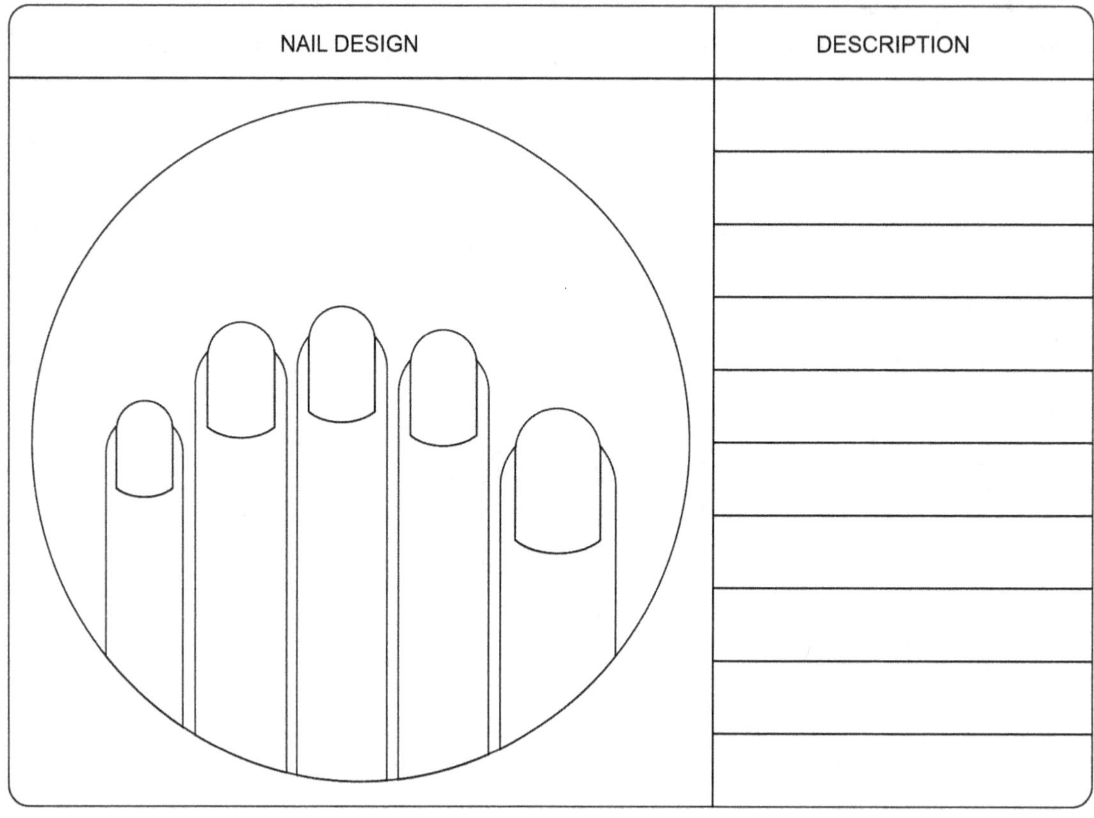

NAIL DESIGN	DESCRIPTION

COLOR PALETTE							
1	2	3	4	5	6	7	8

NR	COLOR	BRAND
1		
2		
3		
4		
5		
6		
7		
8		

DETAILS & PATTERNS

ADDITIONAL NOTES

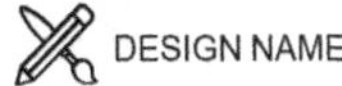 DESIGN NAME ....

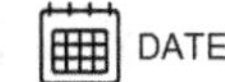 DATE ....

NAIL DESIGN	DESCRIPTION
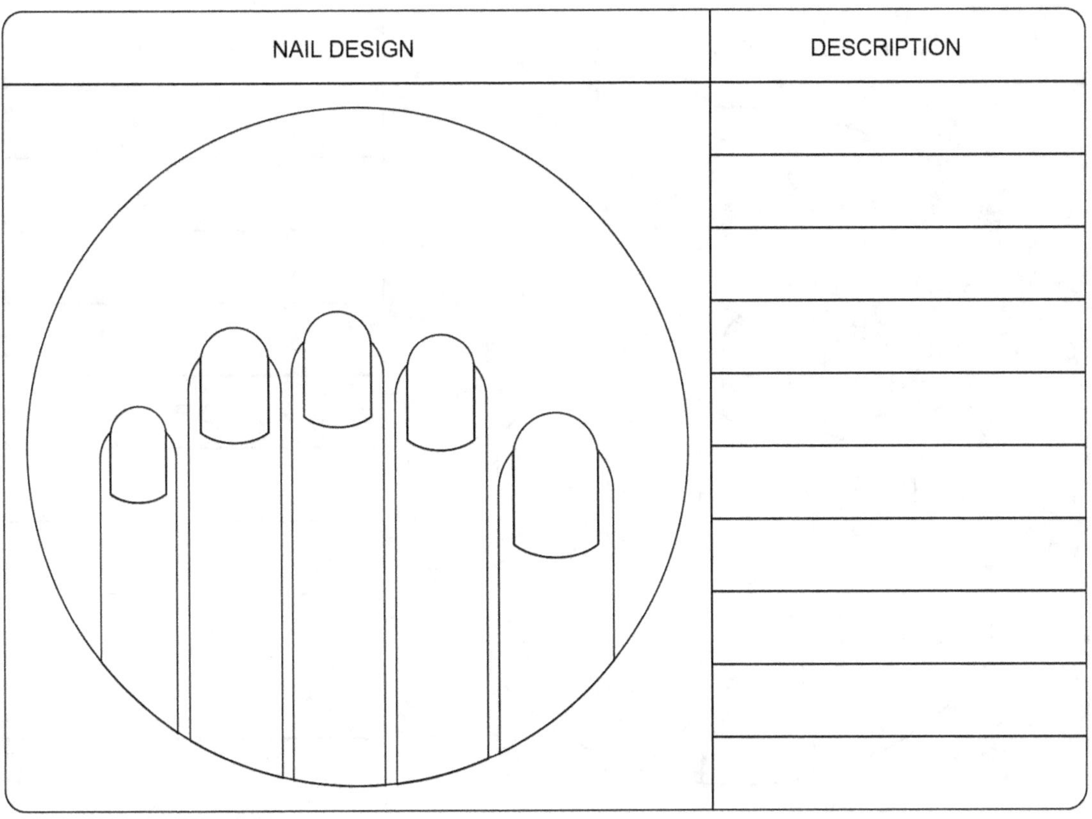	

COLOR PALETTE

1	2	3	4	5	6	7	8

NR	COLOR	BRAND
1		
2		
3		
4		
5		
6		
7		
8		

DETAILS & PATTERNS

ADDITIONAL NOTES

DESIGN NAME .... DATE ....

NAIL DESIGN	DESCRIPTION
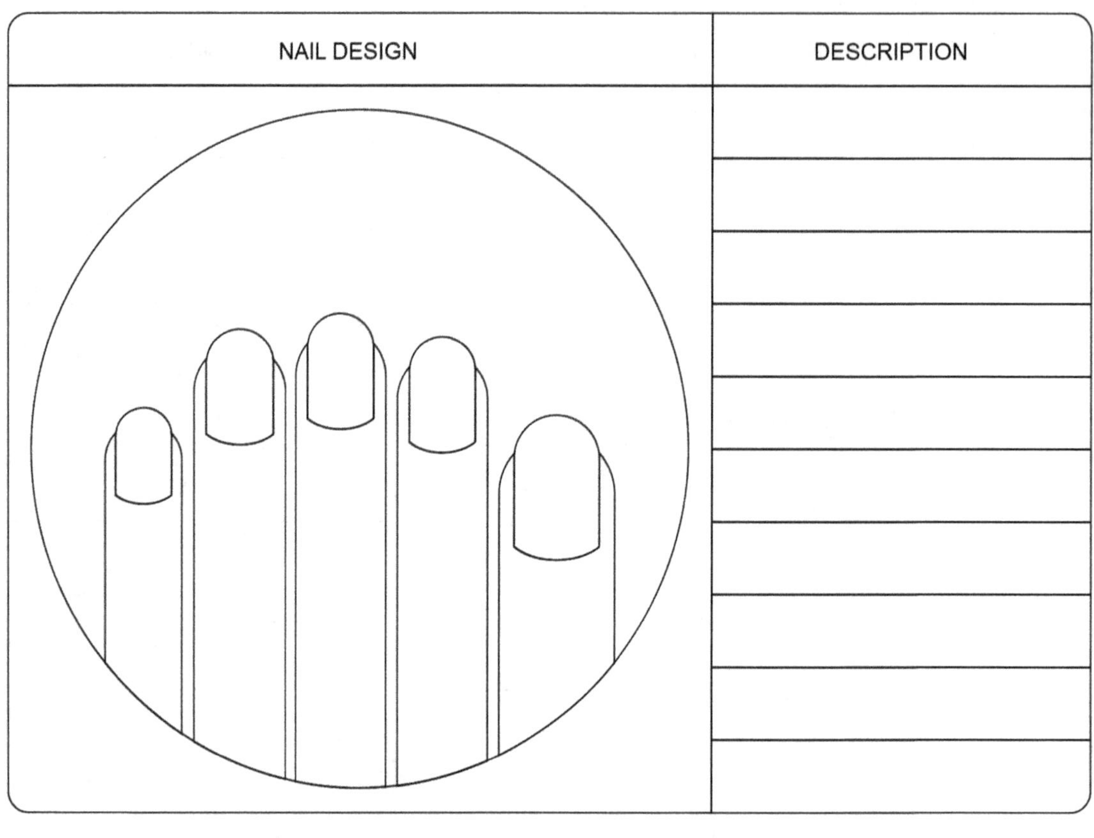	

COLOR PALETTE

1	2	3	4	5	6	7	8

NR	COLOR	BRAND
1		
2		
3		
4		
5		
6		
7		
8		

DETAILS & PATTERNS

ADDITIONAL NOTES

DESIGN NAME .... DATE ....

NAIL DESIGN	DESCRIPTION

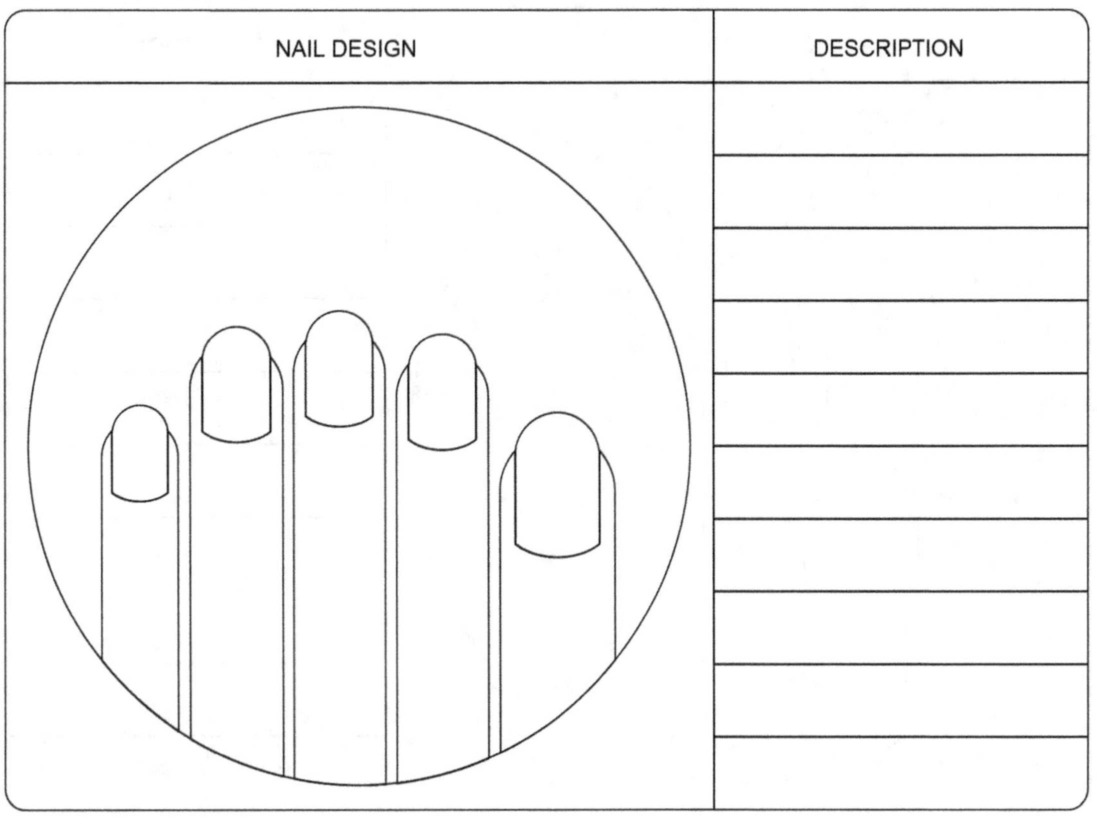

COLOR PALETTE

1	2	3	4	5	6	7	8

NR	COLOR	BRAND
1		
2		
3		
4		
5		
6		
7		
8		

DETAILS & PATTERNS

ADDITIONAL NOTES

DESIGN NAME .... DATE ....

NAIL DESIGN	DESCRIPTION
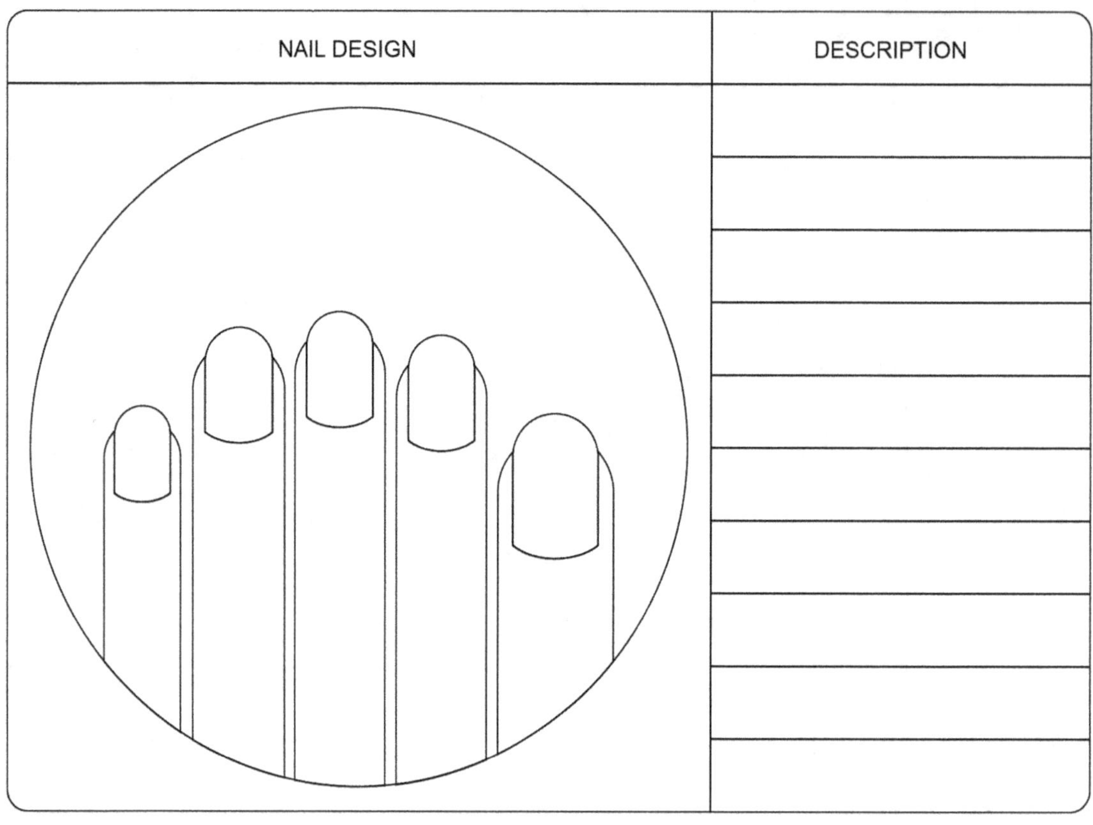	

COLOR PALETTE

1	2	3	4	5	6	7	8

NR	COLOR	BRAND
1		
2		
3		
4		
5		
6		
7		
8		

DETAILS & PATTERNS

ADDITIONAL NOTES

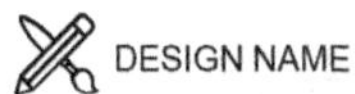 DESIGN NAME ....

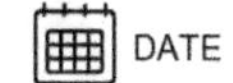 DATE ....

NAIL DESIGN	DESCRIPTION
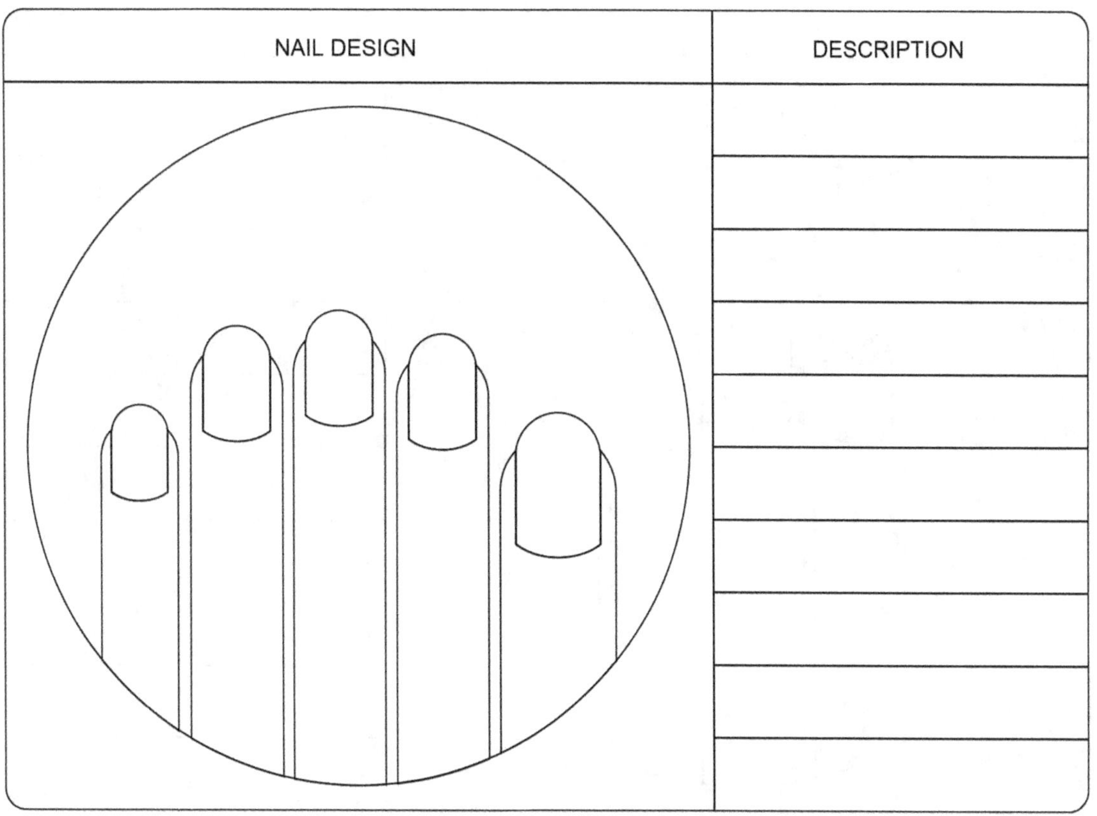	

COLOR PALETTE							
1	2	3	4	5	6	7	8

NR	COLOR	BRAND
1		
2		
3		
4		
5		
6		
7		
8		

DETAILS & PATTERNS

ADDITIONAL NOTES

DESIGN NAME .... DATE ....

NAIL DESIGN	DESCRIPTION
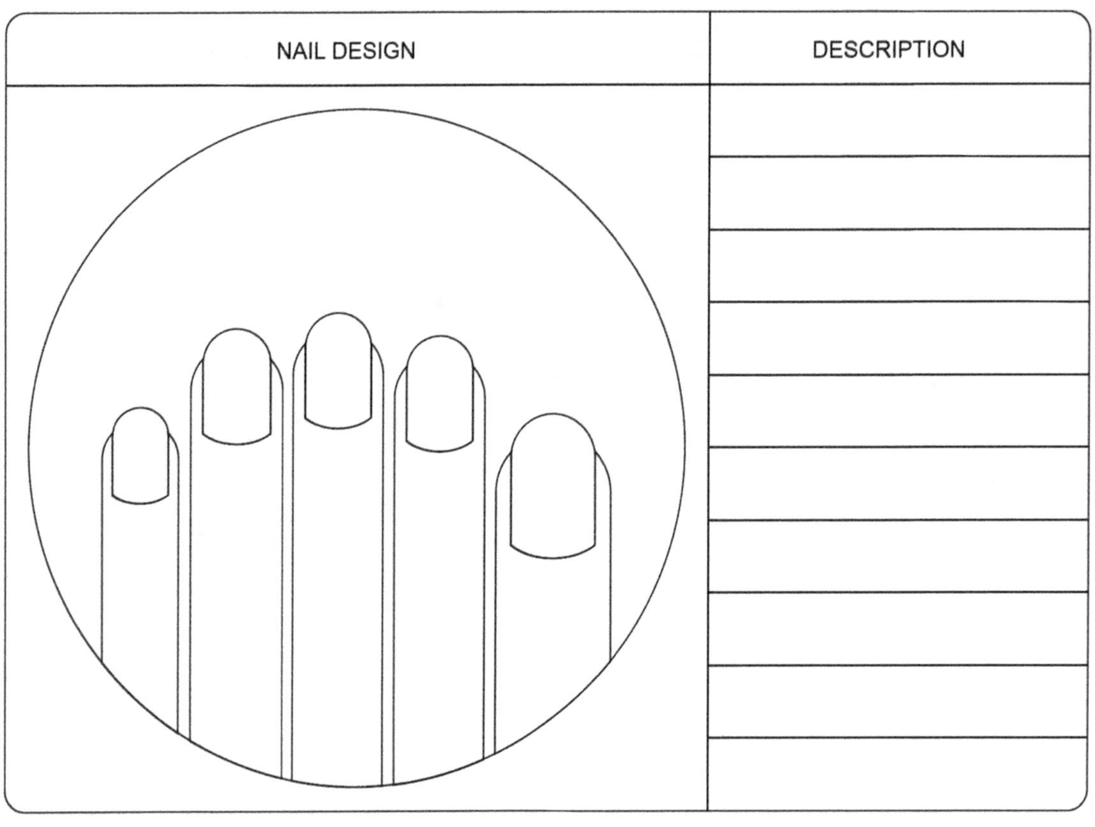	

COLOR PALETTE

1	2	3	4	5	6	7	8

NR	COLOR	BRAND
1		
2		
3		
4		
5		
6		
7		
8		

DETAILS & PATTERNS

ADDITIONAL NOTES

DESIGN NAME .... DATE ....

NAIL DESIGN	DESCRIPTION
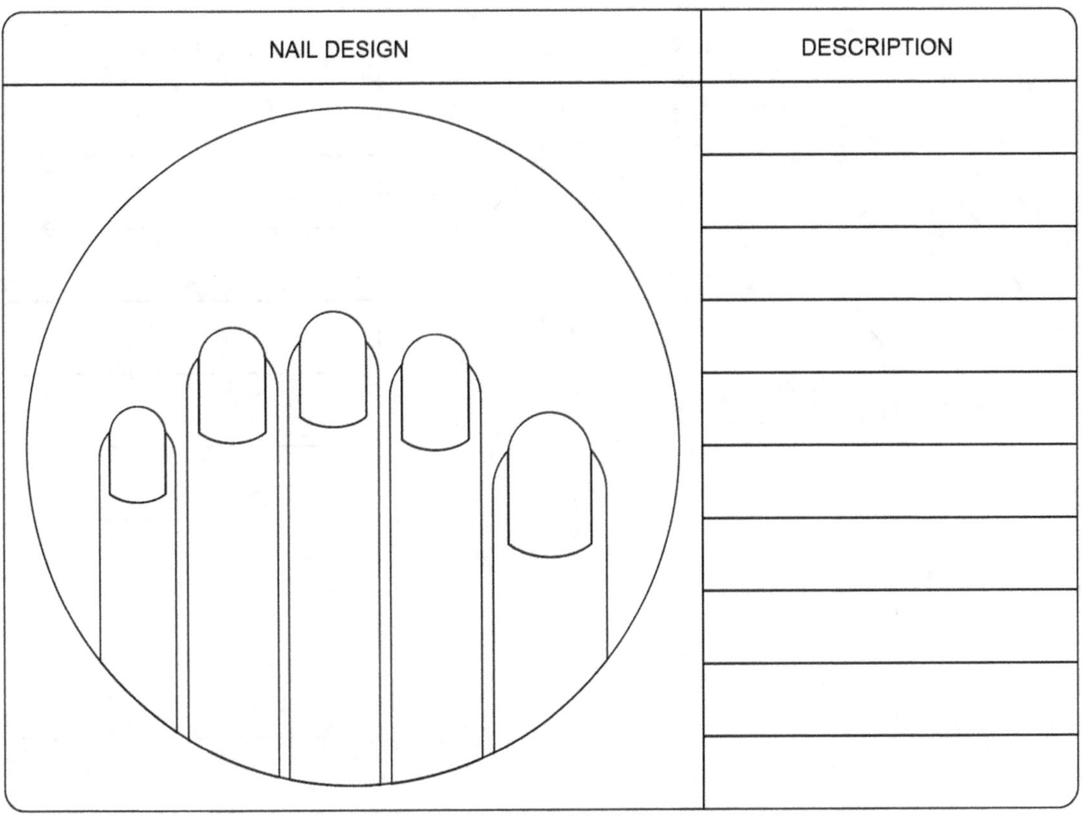	

COLOR PALETTE

1	2	3	4	5	6	7	8

NR	COLOR	BRAND
1		
2		
3		
4		
5		
6		
7		
8		

DETAILS & PATTERNS

ADDITIONAL NOTES

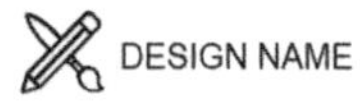 DESIGN NAME ....

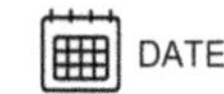 DATE ....

NAIL DESIGN	DESCRIPTION
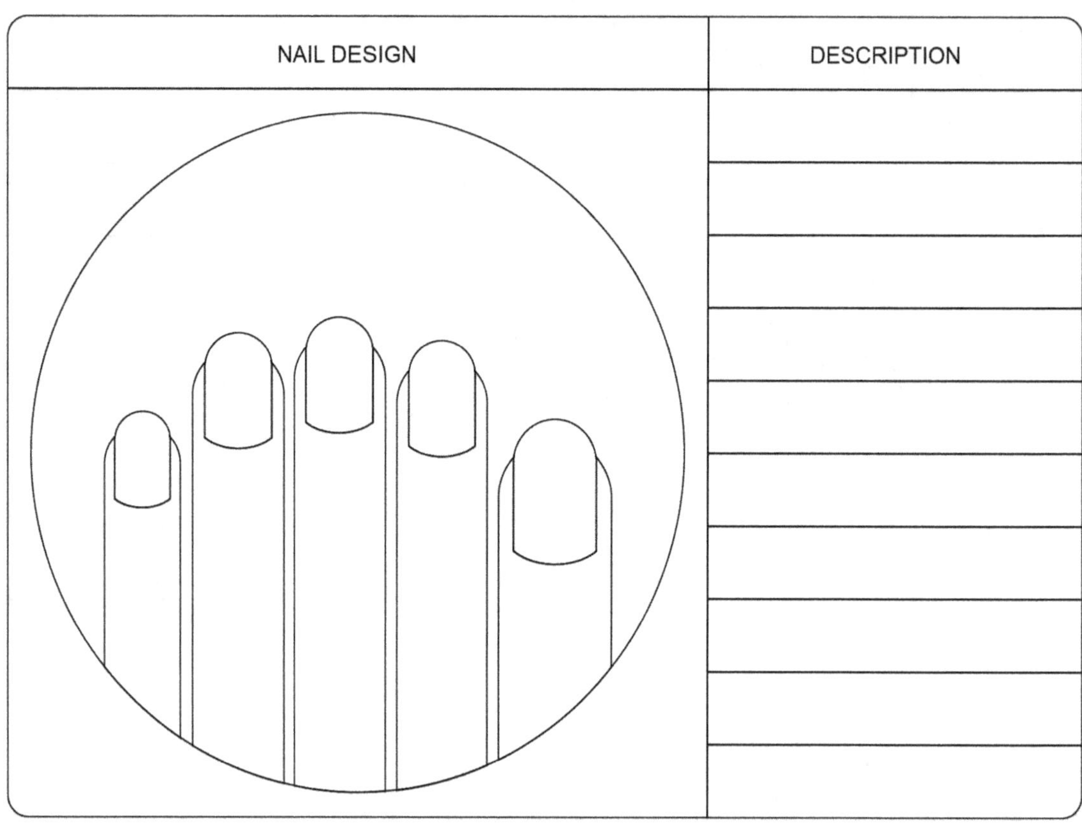	

COLOR PALETTE

1	2	3	4	5	6	7	8

NR	COLOR	BRAND
1		
2		
3		
4		
5		
6		
7		
8		

DETAILS & PATTERNS

ADDITIONAL NOTES

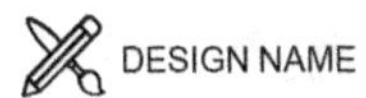 DESIGN NAME ....

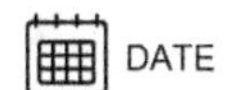 DATE ....

NAIL DESIGN	DESCRIPTION
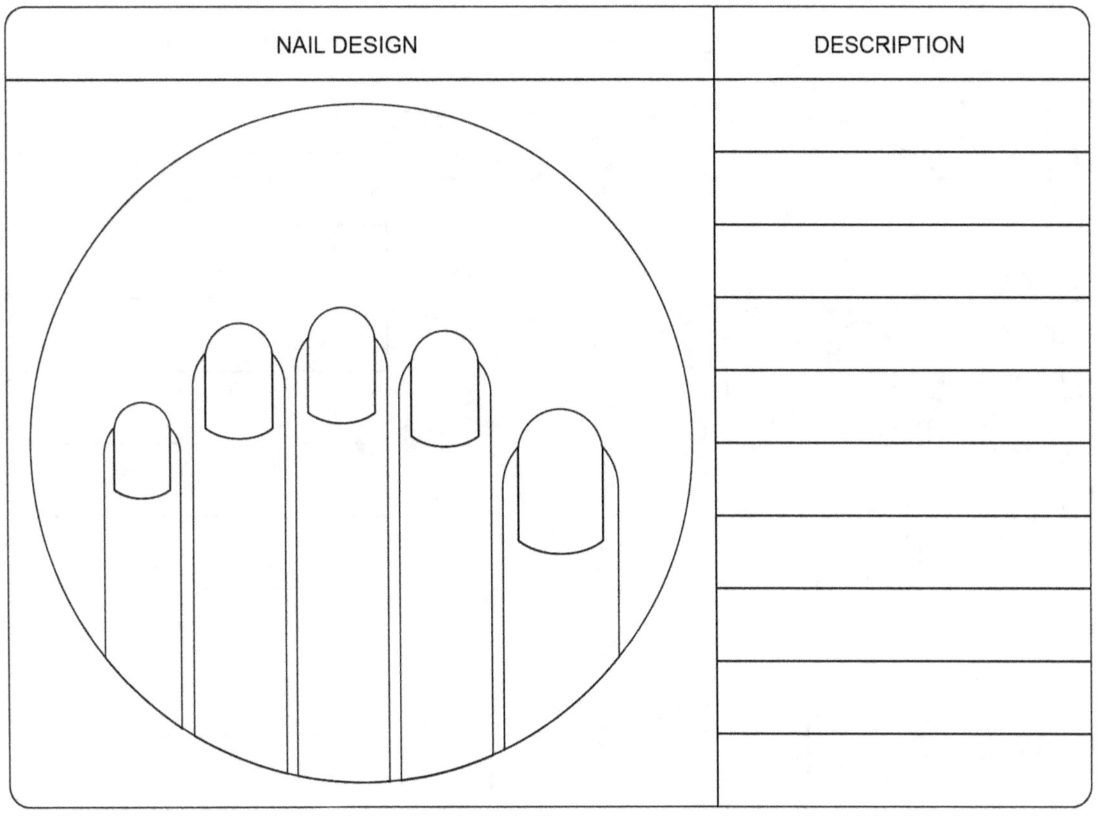	

COLOR PALETTE

1	2	3	4	5	6	7	8

NR	COLOR	BRAND
1		
2		
3		
4		
5		
6		
7		
8		

DETAILS & PATTERNS

ADDITIONAL NOTES

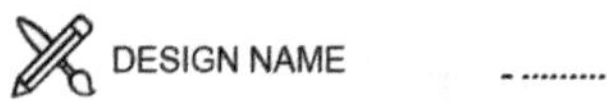

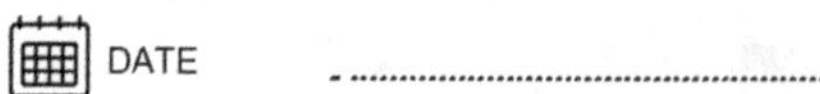

NAIL DESIGN	DESCRIPTION

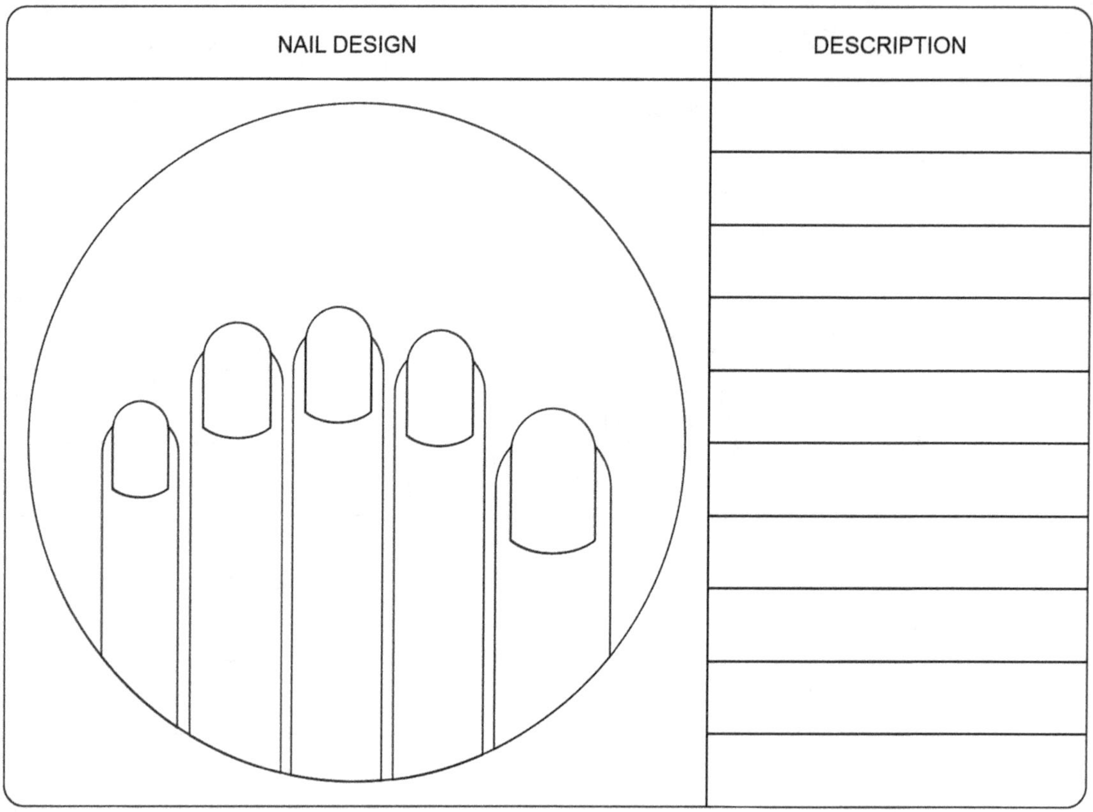

COLOR PALETTE

1	2	3	4	5	6	7	8

NR	COLOR	BRAND
1		
2		
3		
4		
5		
6		
7		
8		

DETAILS & PATTERNS

ADDITIONAL NOTES

DESIGN NAME .... DATE ....

NAIL DESIGN	DESCRIPTION
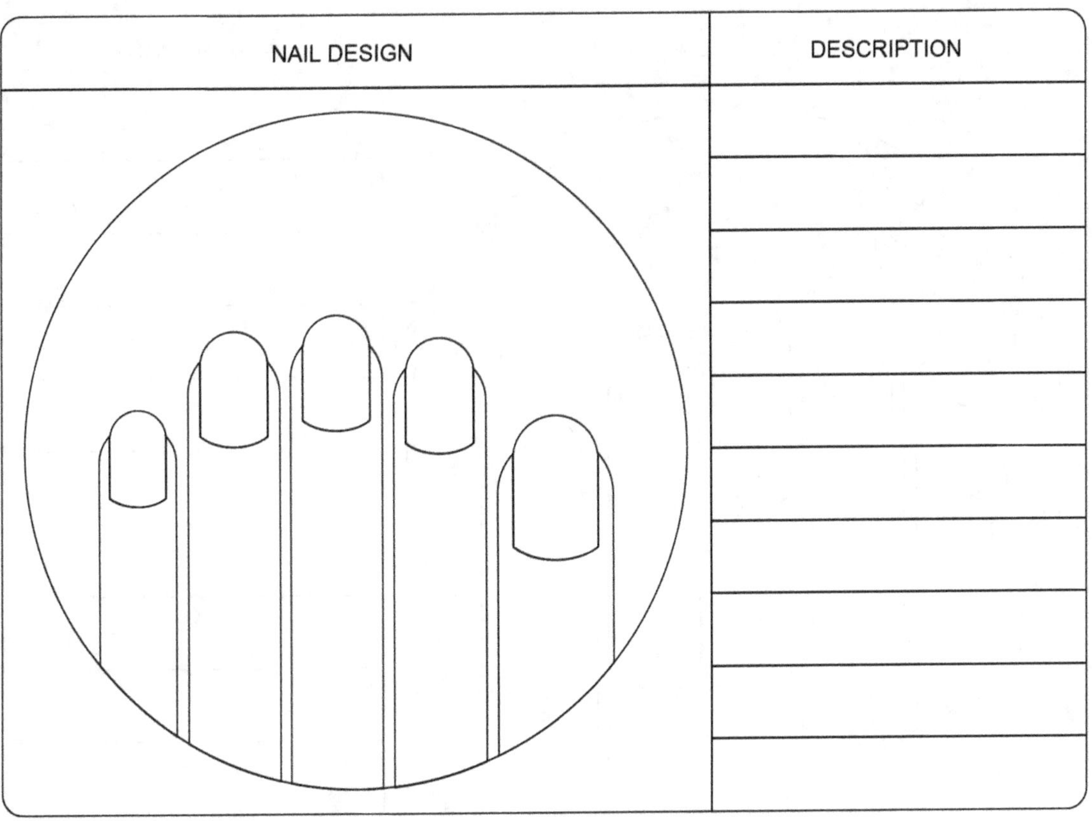	

COLOR PALETTE

1	2	3	4	5	6	7	8

NR	COLOR	BRAND
1		
2		
3		
4		
5		
6		
7		
8		

DETAILS & PATTERNS

ADDITIONAL NOTES

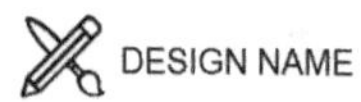 DESIGN NAME ....

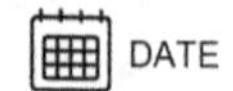 DATE ....

NAIL DESIGN	DESCRIPTION

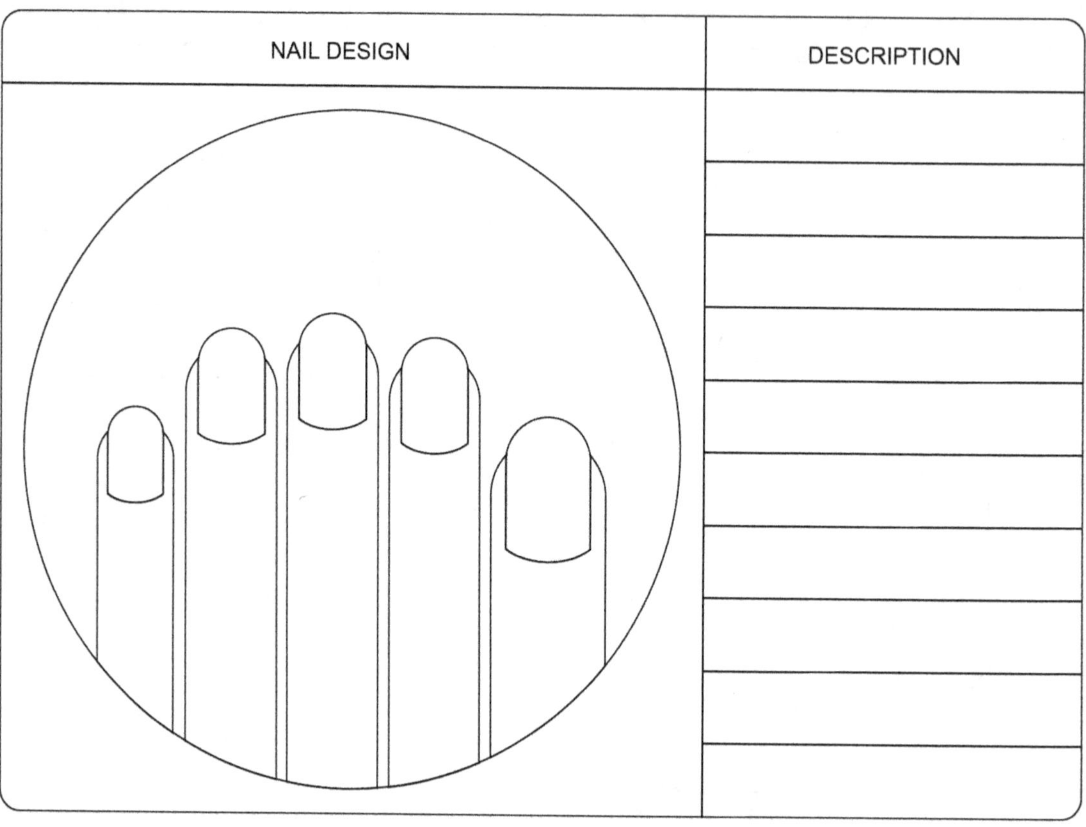

COLOR PALETTE

1	2	3	4	5	6	7	8

NR	COLOR	BRAND
1		
2		
3		
4		
5		
6		
7		
8		

DETAILS & PATTERNS

ADDITIONAL NOTES

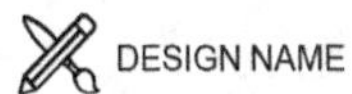
DESIGN NAME ....

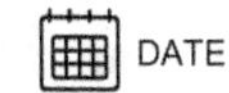
DATE ....

NAIL DESIGN	DESCRIPTION
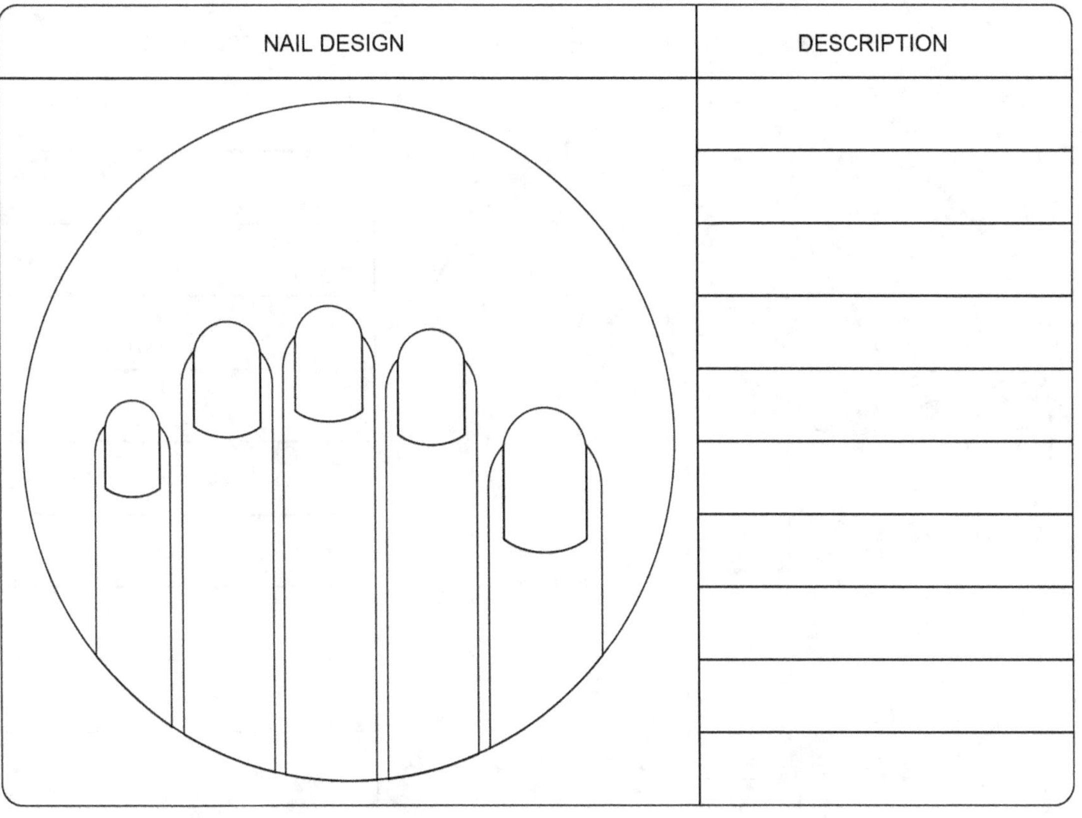	

COLOR PALETTE

1	2	3	4	5	6	7	8

NR	COLOR	BRAND
1		
2		
3		
4		
5		
6		
7		
8		

DETAILS & PATTERNS

ADDITIONAL NOTES

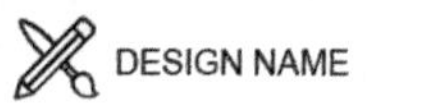

DATE

NAIL DESIGN	DESCRIPTION
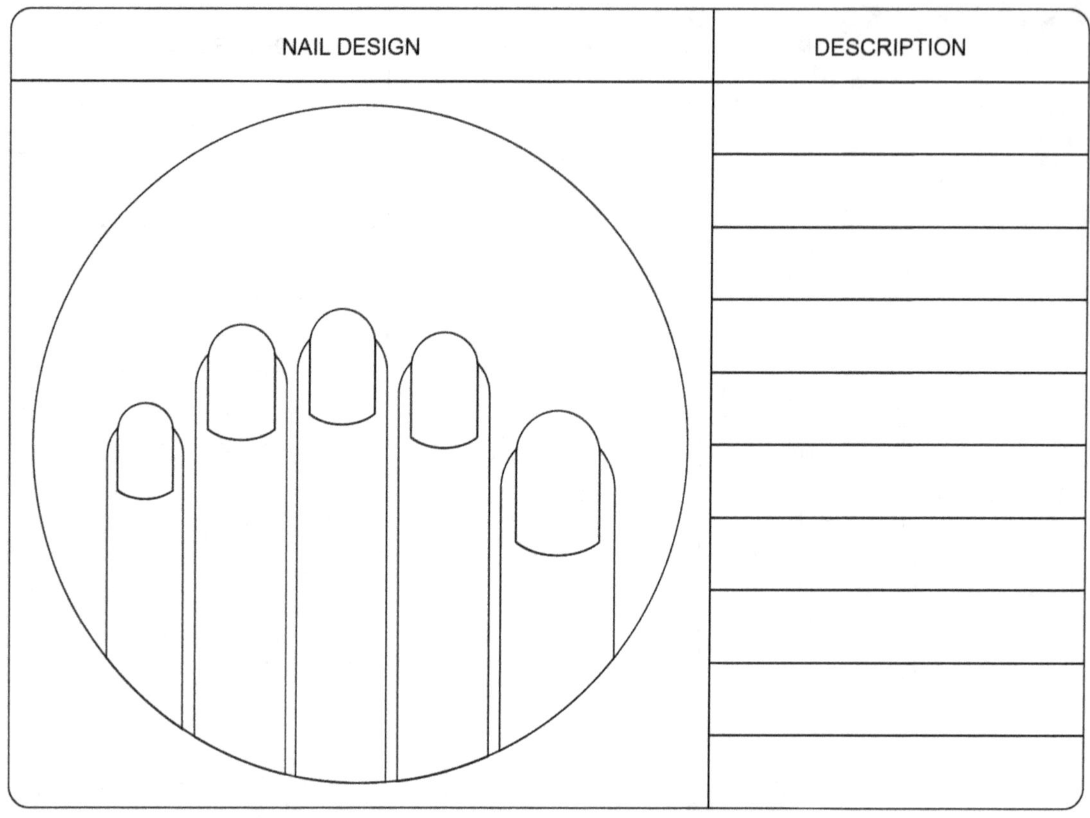	

COLOR PALETTE

1	2	3	4	5	6	7	8

NR	COLOR	BRAND
1		
2		
3		
4		
5		
6		
7		
8		

DETAILS & PATTERNS

ADDITIONAL NOTES

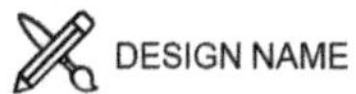 DESIGN NAME ....

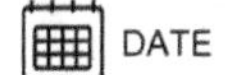 DATE ....

NAIL DESIGN	DESCRIPTION
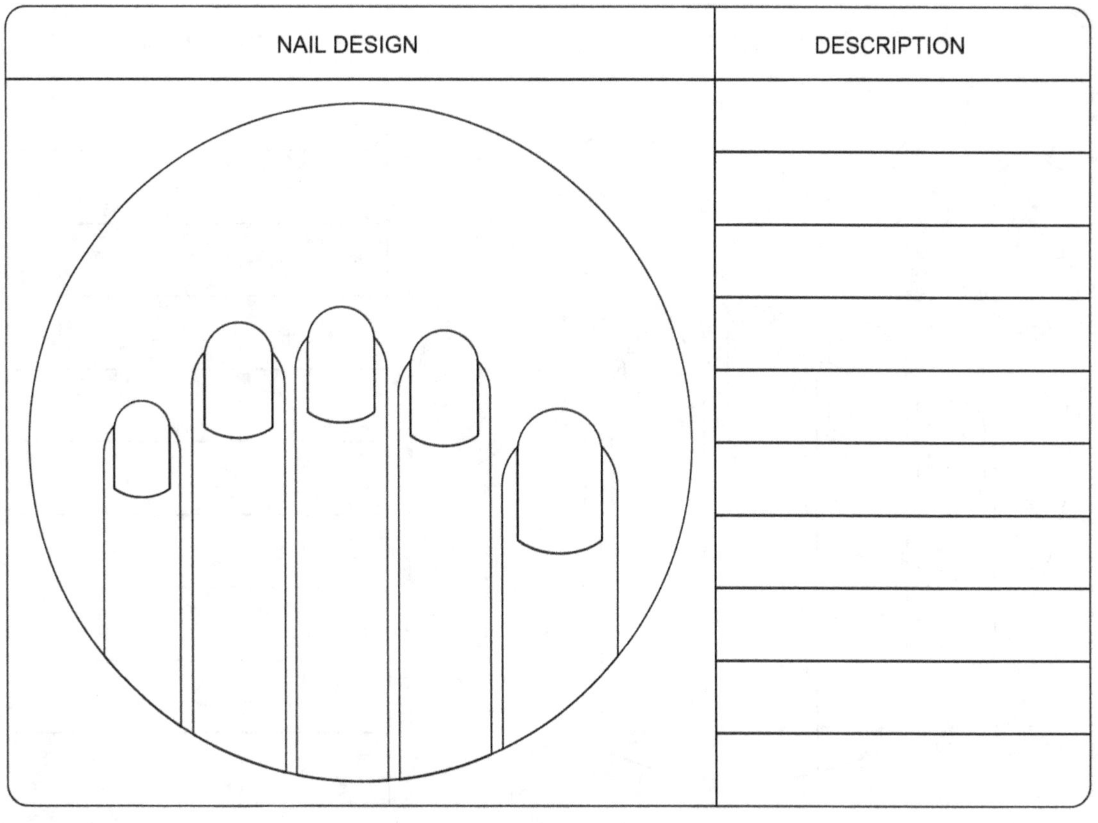	

COLOR PALETTE

1	2	3	4	5	6	7	8

NR	COLOR	BRAND
1		
2		
3		
4		
5		
6		
7		
8		

DETAILS & PATTERNS

ADDITIONAL NOTES

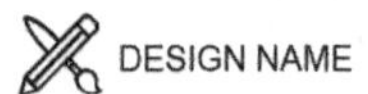

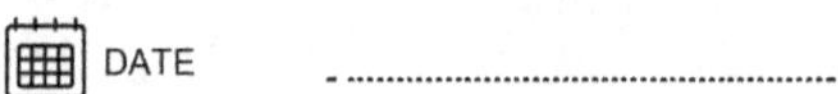

NAIL DESIGN	DESCRIPTION

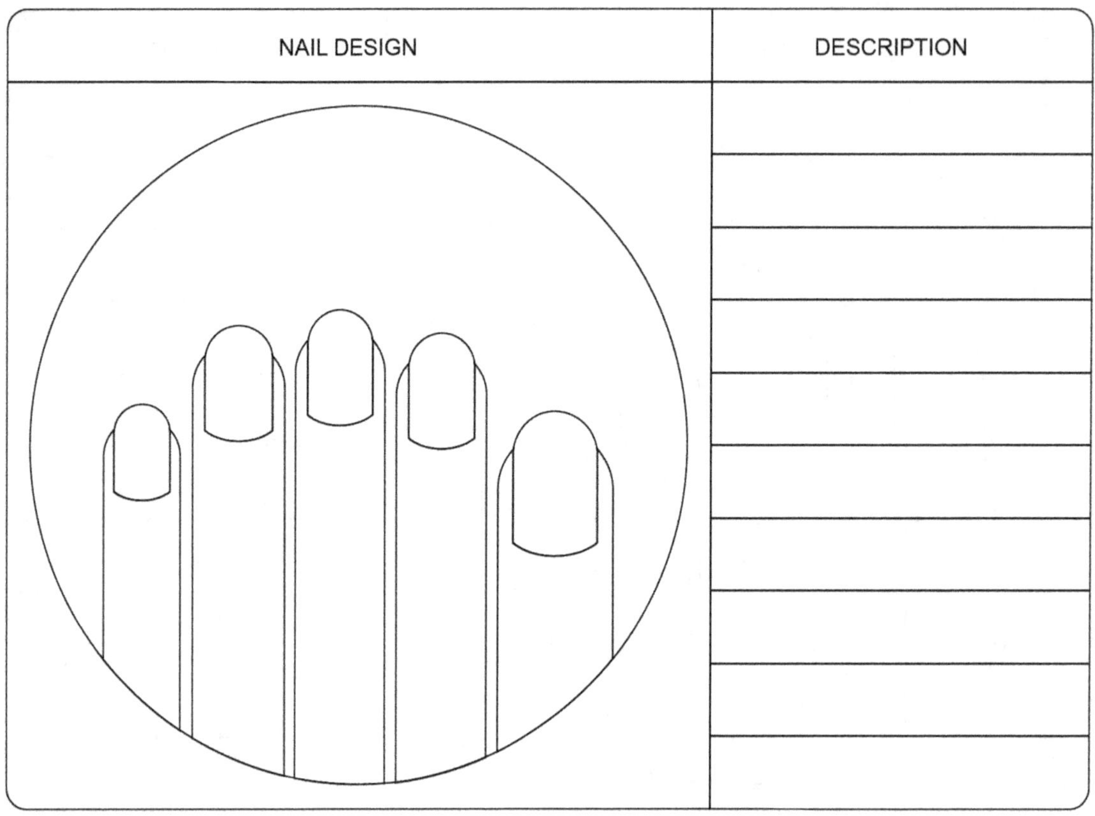

COLOR PALETTE							
1	2	3	4	5	6	7	8

NR	COLOR	BRAND
1		
2		
3		
4		
5		
6		
7		
8		

DETAILS & PATTERNS

ADDITIONAL NOTES

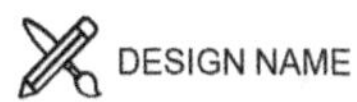

DESIGN NAME .... DATE ....

NAIL DESIGN	DESCRIPTION
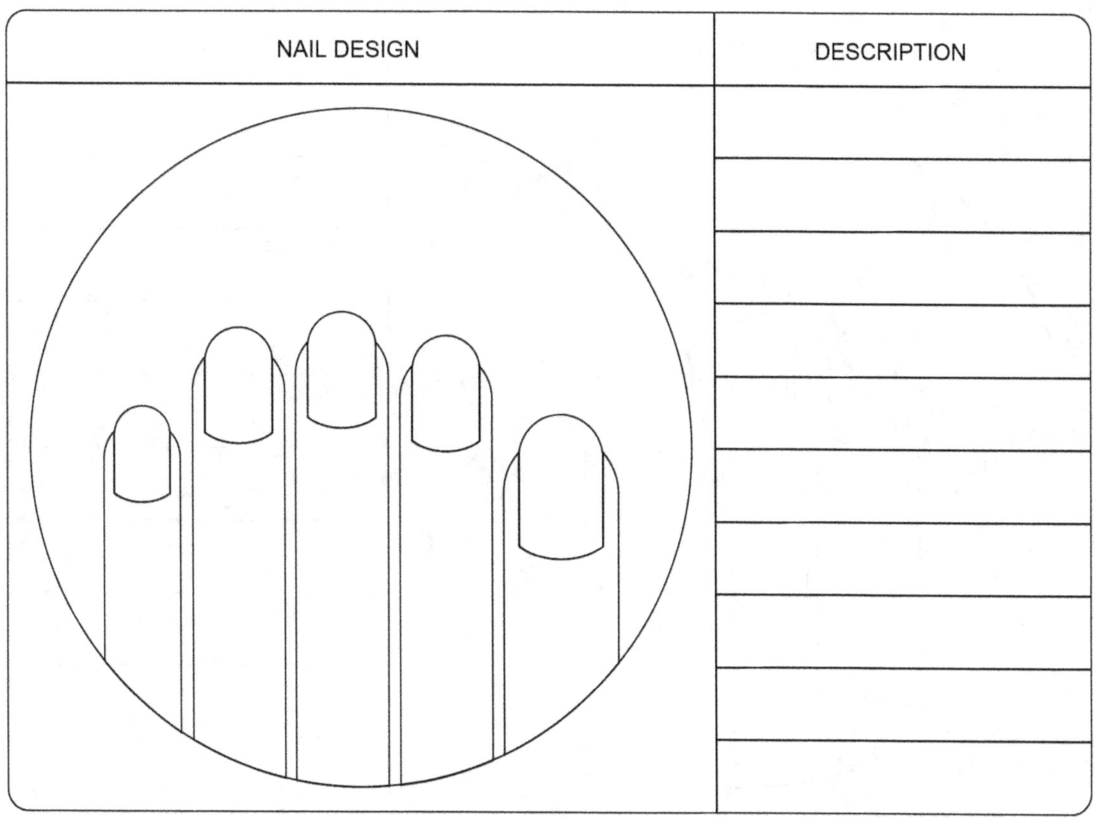	

COLOR PALETTE

1	2	3	4	5	6	7	8

NR	COLOR	BRAND
1		
2		
3		
4		
5		
6		
7		
8		

DETAILS & PATTERNS

ADDITIONAL NOTES

DESIGN NAME ....

DATE ....

NAIL DESIGN	DESCRIPTION
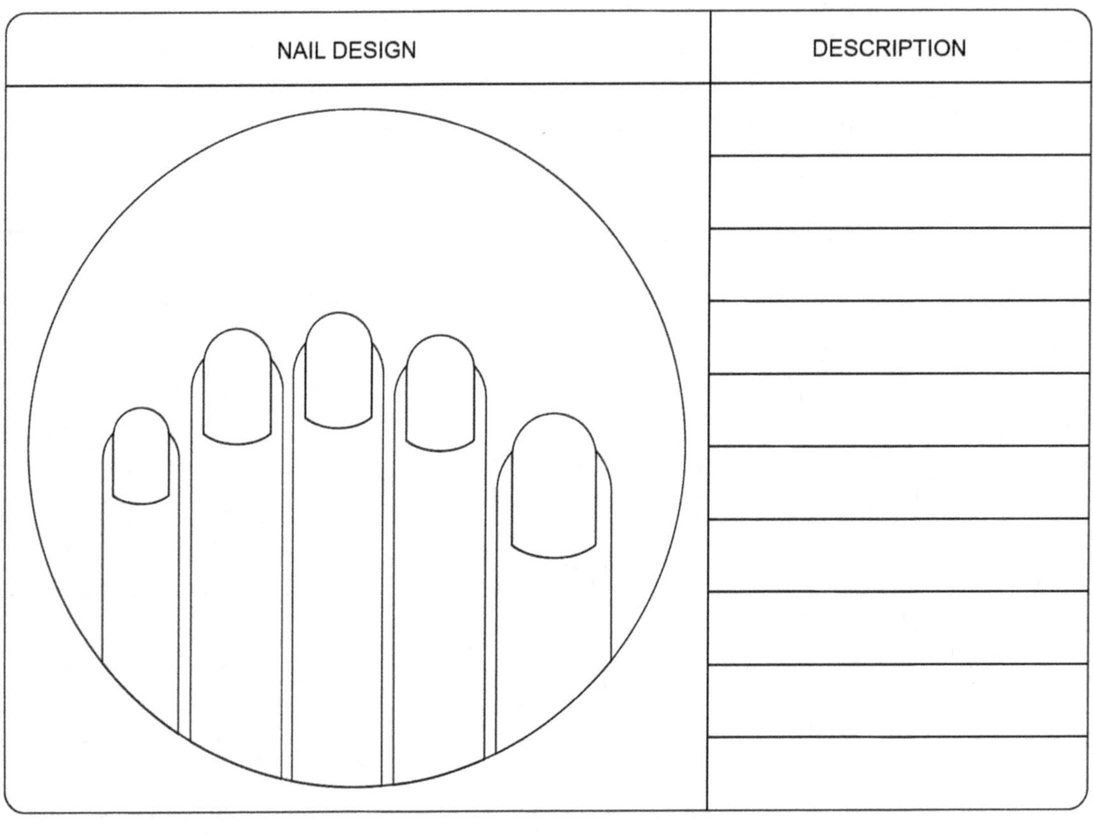	

COLOR PALETTE

1	2	3	4	5	6	7	8

NR	COLOR	BRAND
1		
2		
3		
4		
5		
6		
7		
8		

DETAILS & PATTERNS

ADDITIONAL NOTES

DESIGN NAME .... DATE ....

NAIL DESIGN	DESCRIPTION
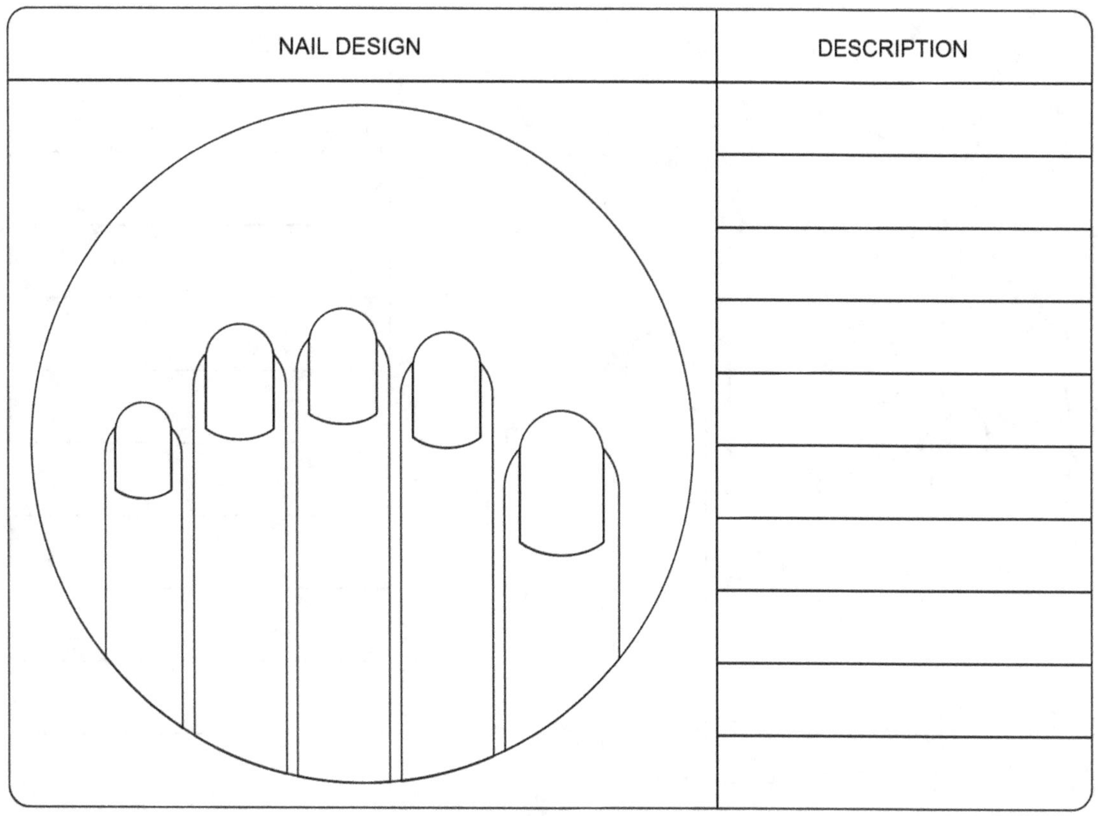	

COLOR PALETTE

1	2	3	4	5	6	7	8

NR	COLOR	BRAND
1		
2		
3		
4		
5		
6		
7		
8		

DETAILS & PATTERNS

ADDITIONAL NOTES

DESIGN NAME .... DATE ....

NAIL DESIGN	DESCRIPTION

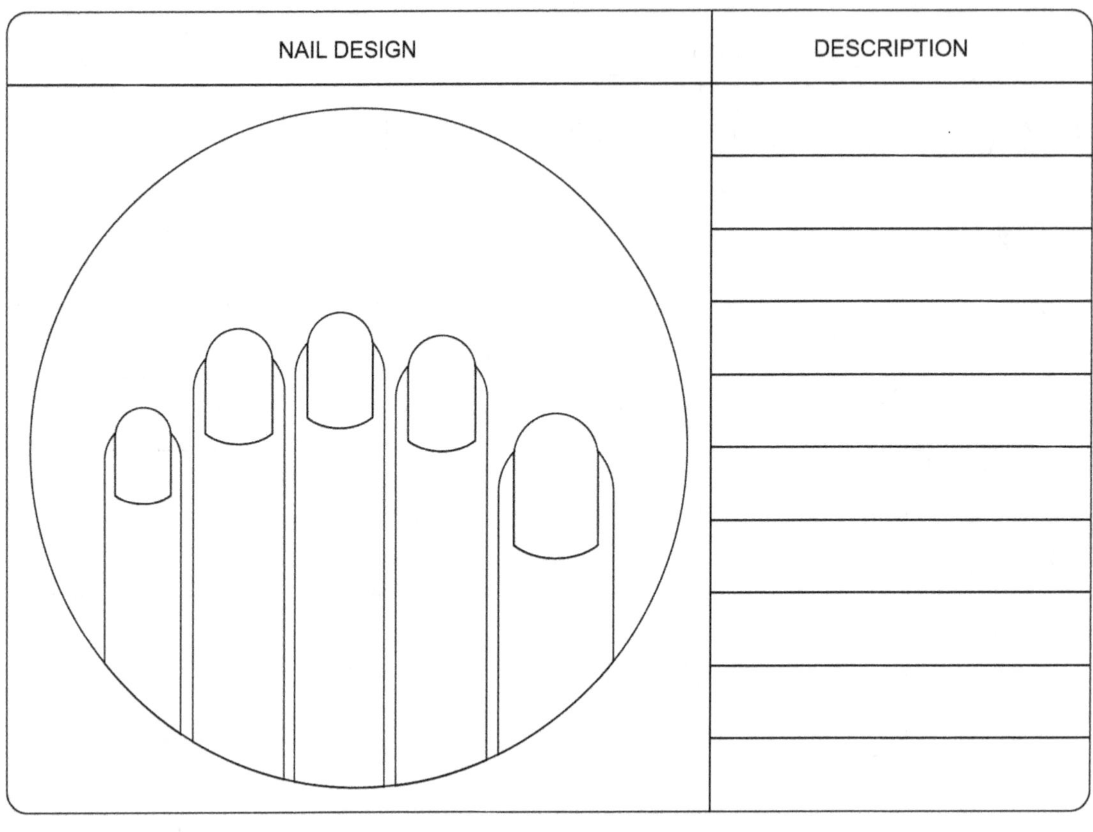

COLOR PALETTE

1	2	3	4	5	6	7	8

NR	COLOR	BRAND
1		
2		
3		
4		
5		
6		
7		
8		

DETAILS & PATTERNS

ADDITIONAL NOTES

DESIGN NAME ....   DATE ....

NAIL DESIGN	DESCRIPTION

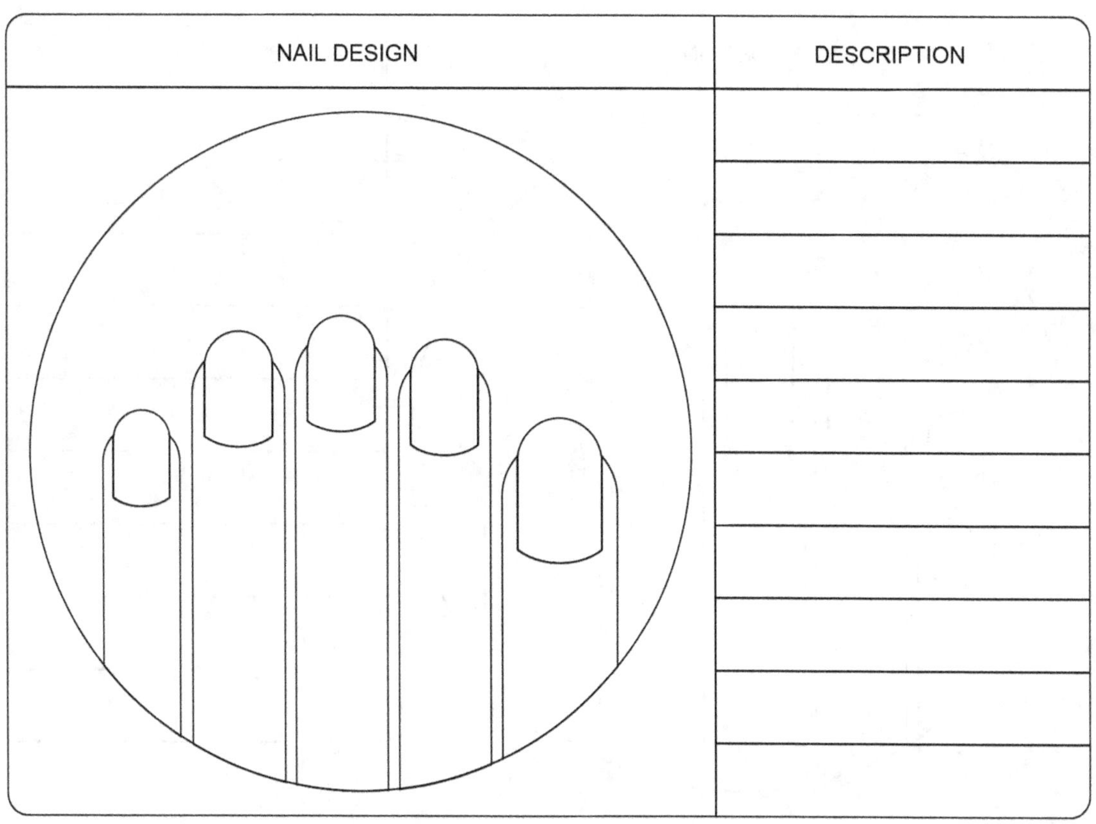

COLOR PALETTE

1	2	3	4	5	6	7	8

NR	COLOR	BRAND
1		
2		
3		
4		
5		
6		
7		
8		

DETAILS & PATTERNS

ADDITIONAL NOTES

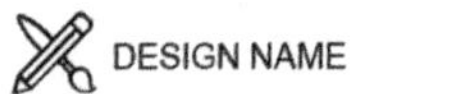

DESIGN NAME ....

DATE ....

NAIL DESIGN	DESCRIPTION
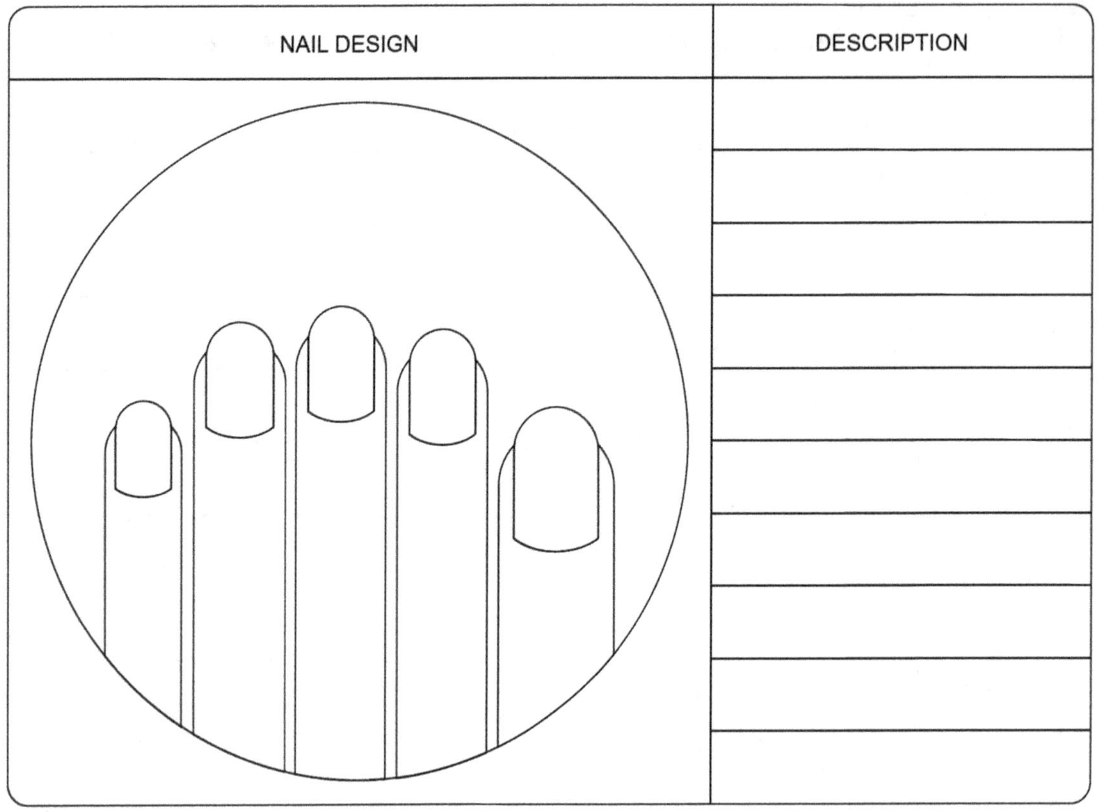	

COLOR PALETTE							
1	2	3	4	5	6	7	8

NR	COLOR	BRAND
1		
2		
3		
4		
5		
6		
7		
8		

DETAILS & PATTERNS

ADDITIONAL NOTES

DESIGN NAME .... DATE ....

NAIL DESIGN	DESCRIPTION
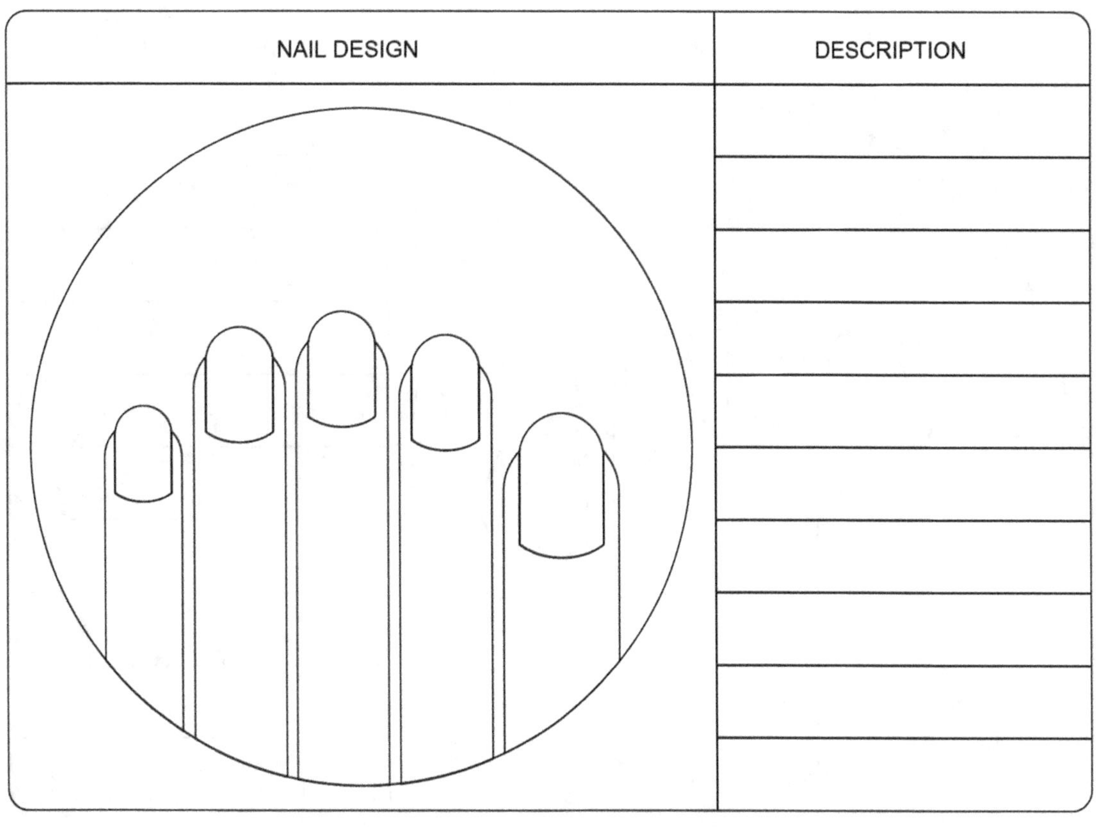	

COLOR PALETTE							
1	2	3	4	5	6	7	8

NR	COLOR	BRAND
1		
2		
3		
4		
5		
6		
7		
8		

DETAILS & PATTERNS

ADDITIONAL NOTES

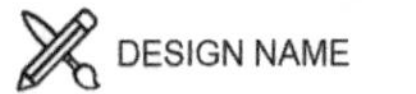

DESIGN NAME .... DATE ....

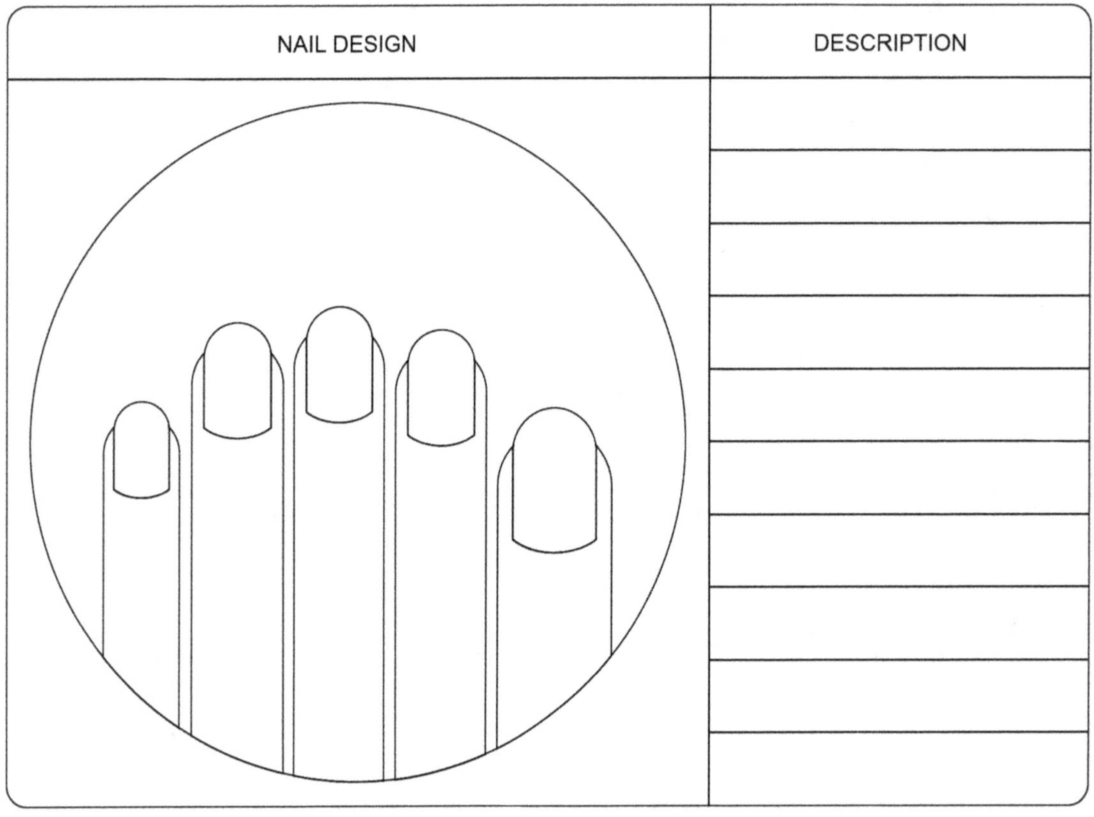

NAIL DESIGN	DESCRIPTION

COLOR PALETTE

1	2	3	4	5	6	7	8

NR	COLOR	BRAND
1		
2		
3		
4		
5		
6		
7		
8		

DETAILS & PATTERNS

ADDITIONAL NOTES

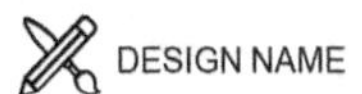
DESIGN NAME ....

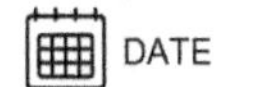
DATE ....

NAIL DESIGN	DESCRIPTION

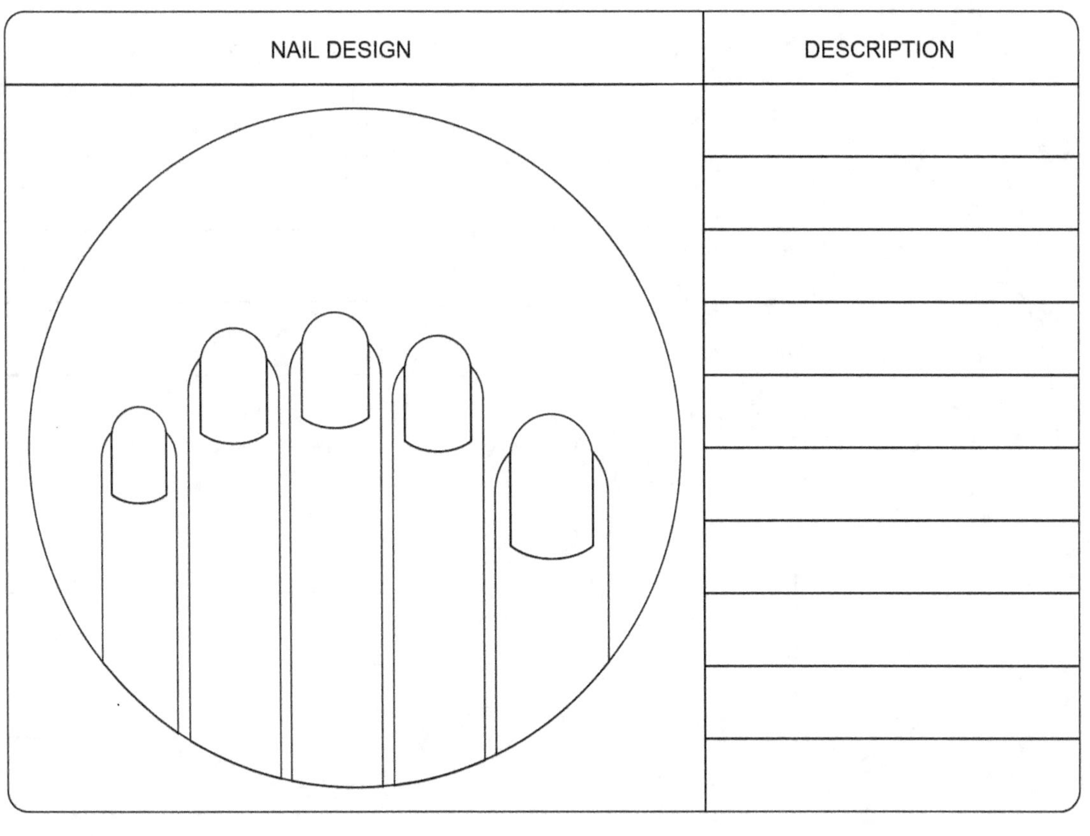

COLOR PALETTE

1	2	3	4	5	6	7	8

NR	COLOR	BRAND
1		
2		
3		
4		
5		
6		
7		
8		

DETAILS & PATTERNS

ADDITIONAL NOTES

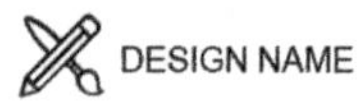
DESIGN NAME ....

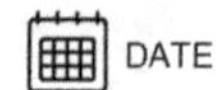
DATE ....

NAIL DESIGN	DESCRIPTION
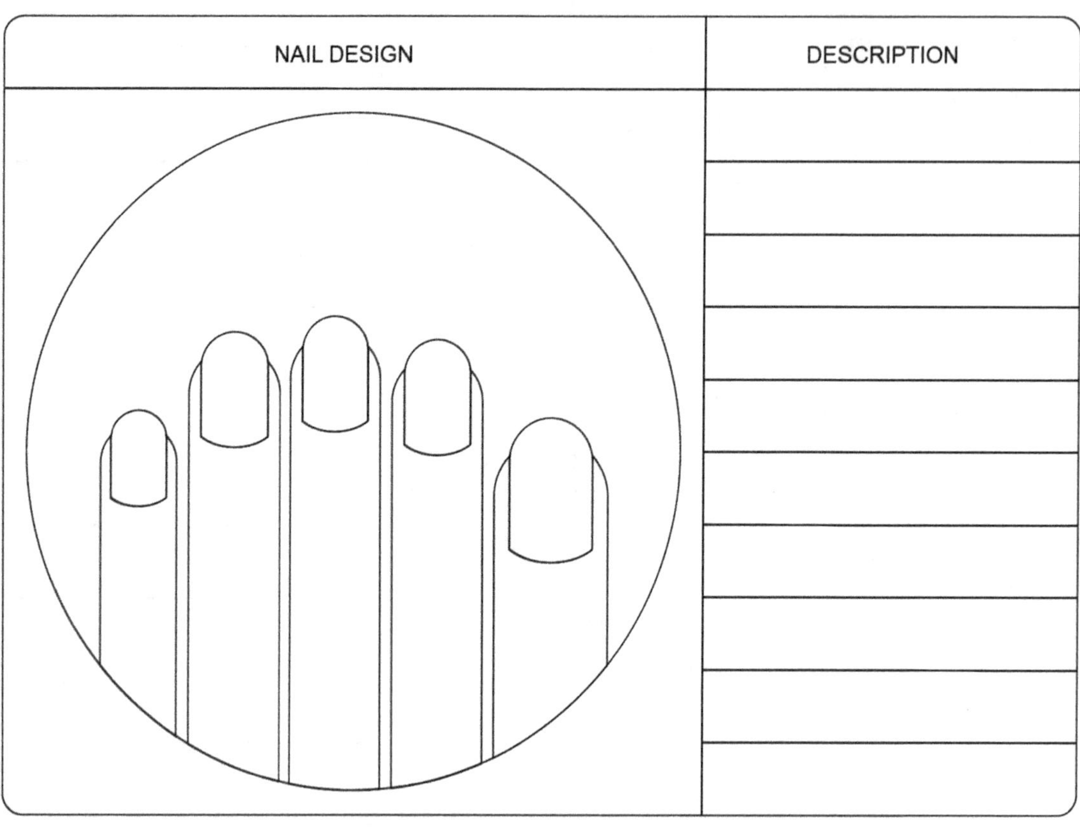	

COLOR PALETTE

1	2	3	4	5	6	7	8

NR	COLOR	BRAND
1		
2		
3		
4		
5		
6		
7		
8		

DETAILS & PATTERNS

ADDITIONAL NOTES

DESIGN NAME .... DATE ....

NAIL DESIGN	DESCRIPTION

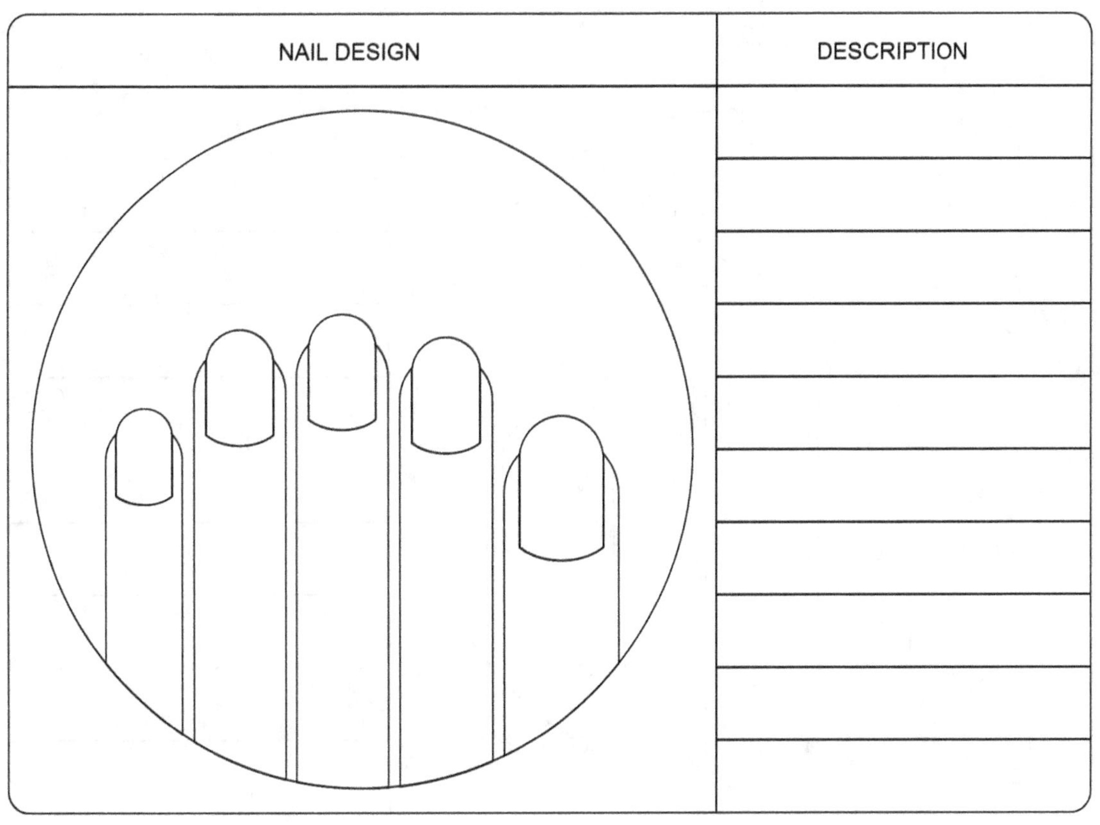

COLOR PALETTE

1	2	3	4	5	6	7	8

NR	COLOR	BRAND
1		
2		
3		
4		
5		
6		
7		
8		

DETAILS & PATTERNS

ADDITIONAL NOTES

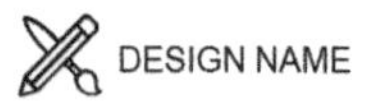

DESIGN NAME ....

DATE ....

NAIL DESIGN	DESCRIPTION

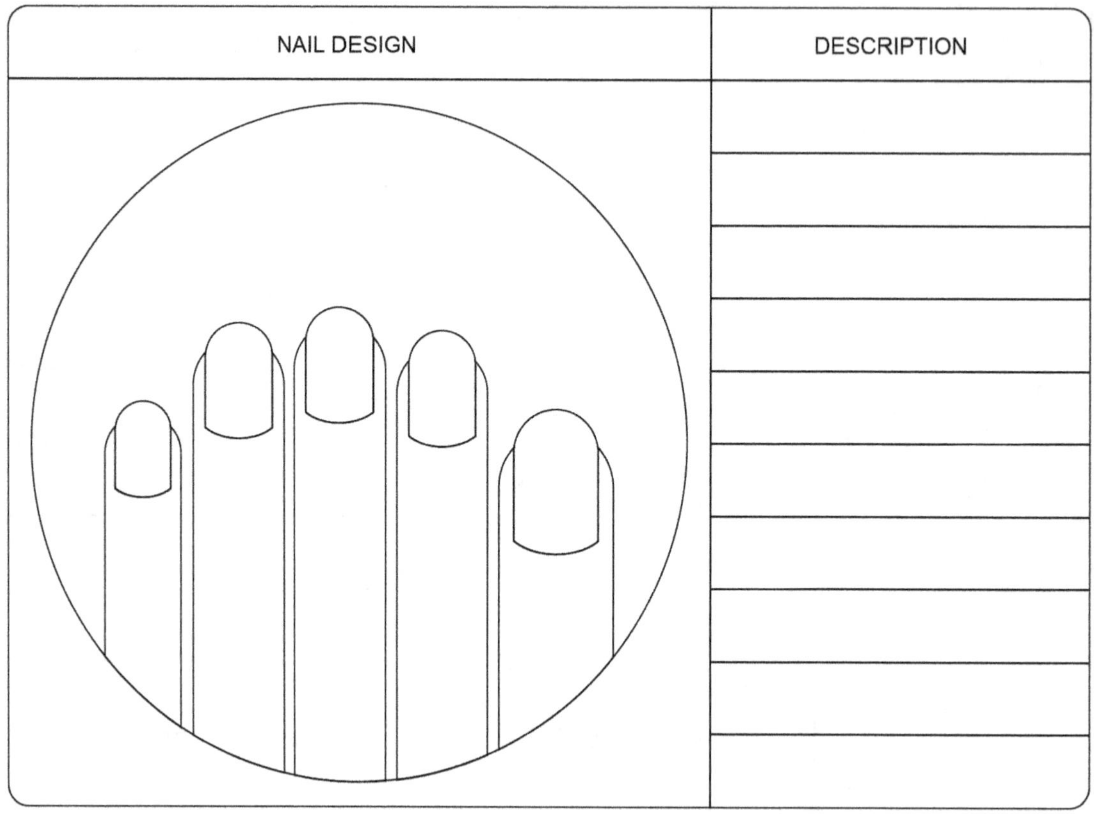

COLOR PALETTE

1	2	3	4	5	6	7	8

NR	COLOR	BRAND
1		
2		
3		
4		
5		
6		
7		
8		

DETAILS & PATTERNS

ADDITIONAL NOTES

DESIGN NAME ....

DATE ....

NAIL DESIGN	DESCRIPTION
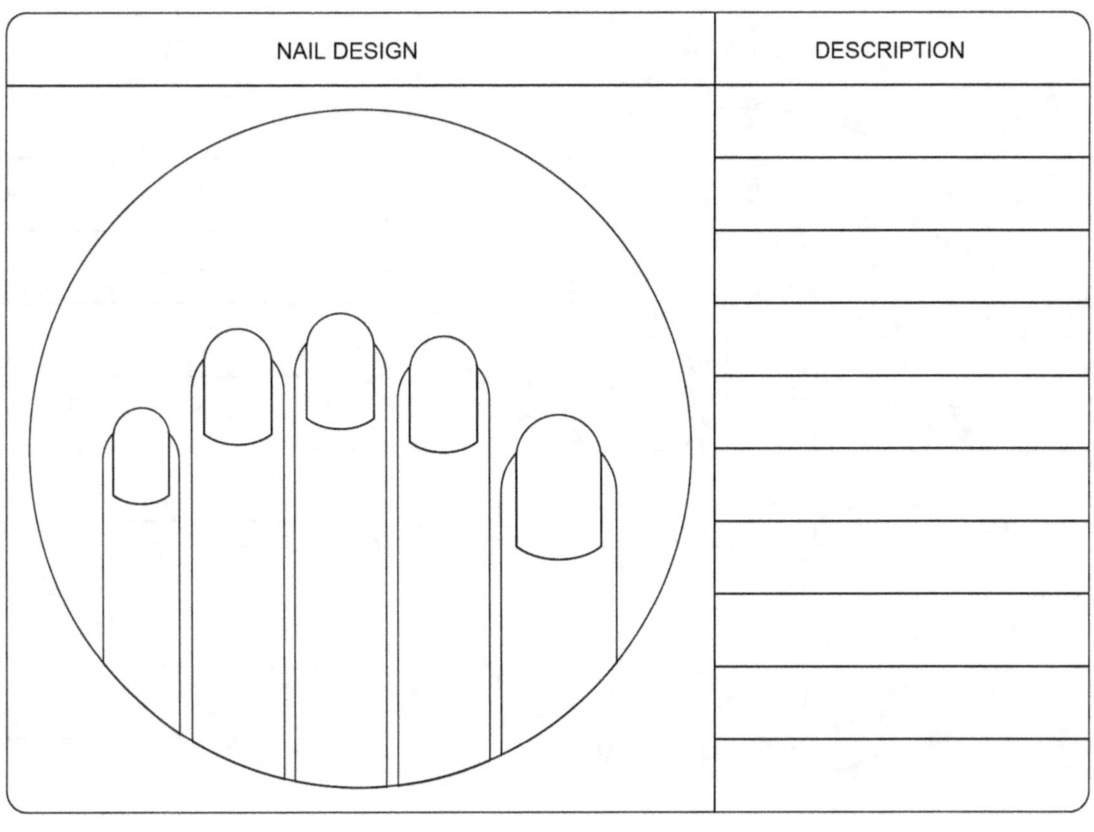	

COLOR PALETTE

1	2	3	4	5	6	7	8

NR	COLOR	BRAND
1		
2		
3		
4		
5		
6		
7		
8		

DETAILS & PATTERNS

ADDITIONAL NOTES

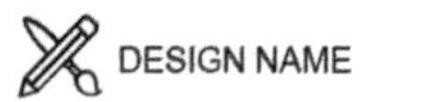

DATE ....

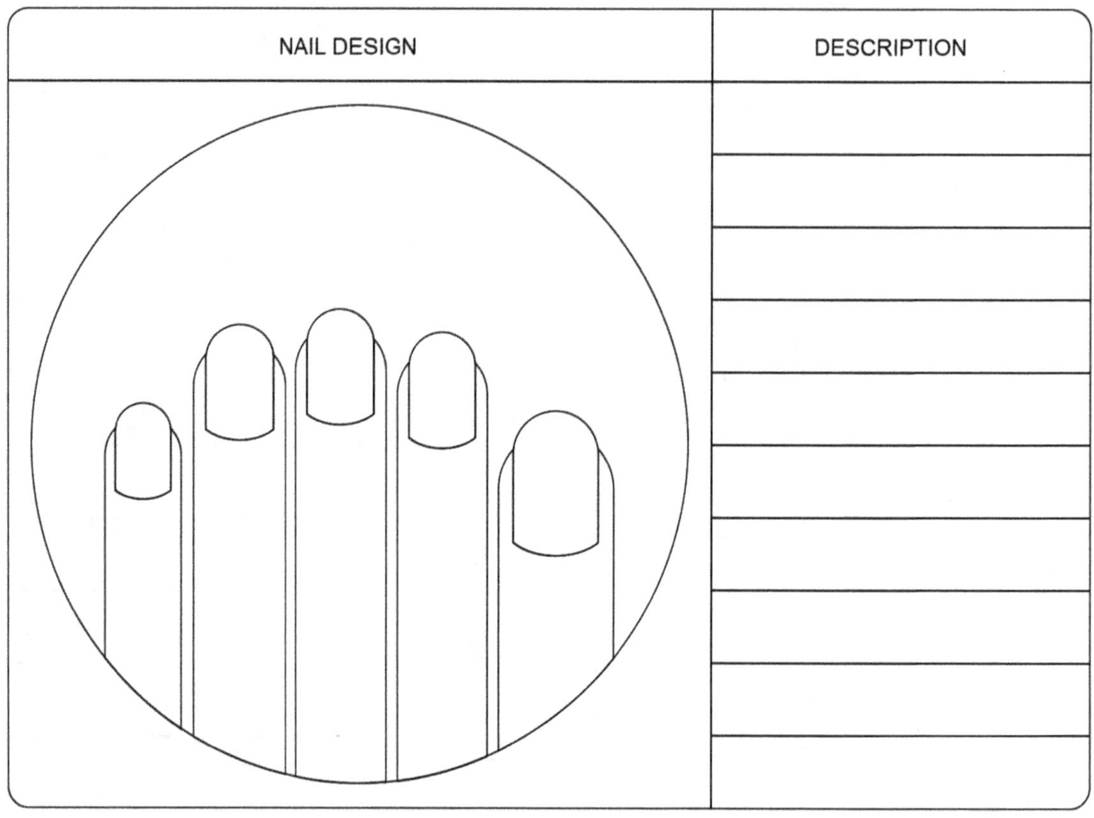

COLOR PALETTE

1	2	3	4	5	6	7	8

NR	COLOR	BRAND
1		
2		
3		
4		
5		
6		
7		
8		

DETAILS & PATTERNS

ADDITIONAL NOTES

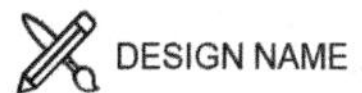 DESIGN NAME ....

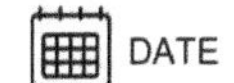 DATE ....

NAIL DESIGN	DESCRIPTION
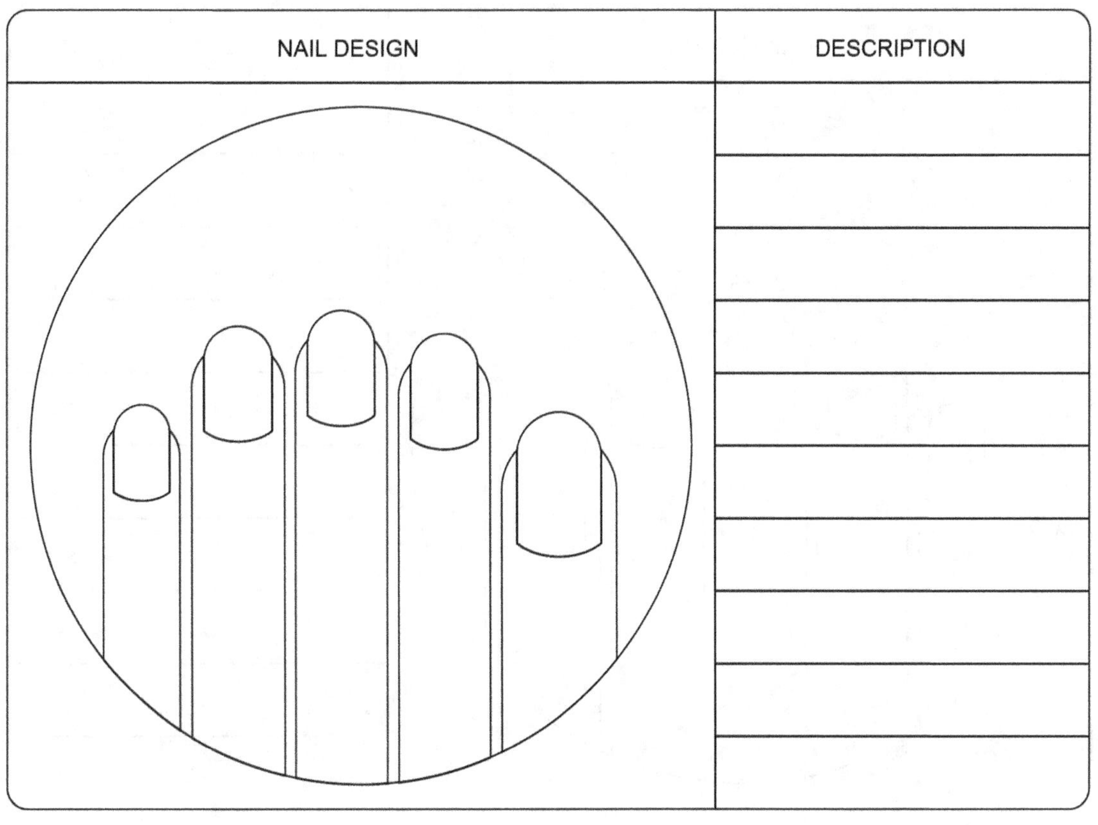	

COLOR PALETTE

1	2	3	4	5	6	7	8

NR	COLOR	BRAND
1		
2		
3		
4		
5		
6		
7		
8		

DETAILS & PATTERNS

ADDITIONAL NOTES

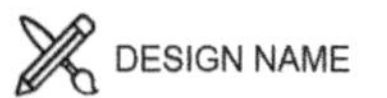

DESIGN NAME .... DATE ....

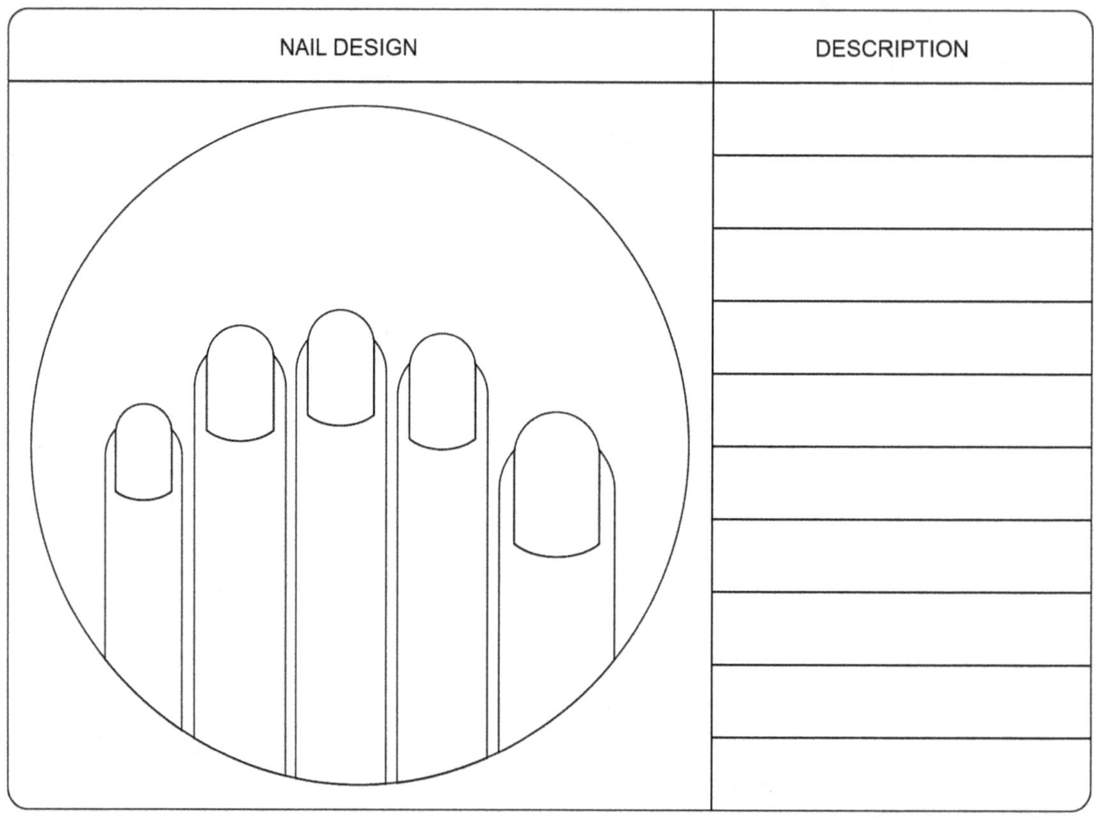

COLOR PALETTE

1	2	3	4	5	6	7	8

NR	COLOR	BRAND
1		
2		
3		
4		
5		
6		
7		
8		

DETAILS & PATTERNS

ADDITIONAL NOTES

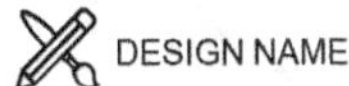
DESIGN NAME ....

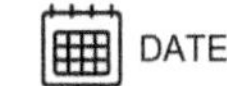
DATE ....

NAIL DESIGN	DESCRIPTION
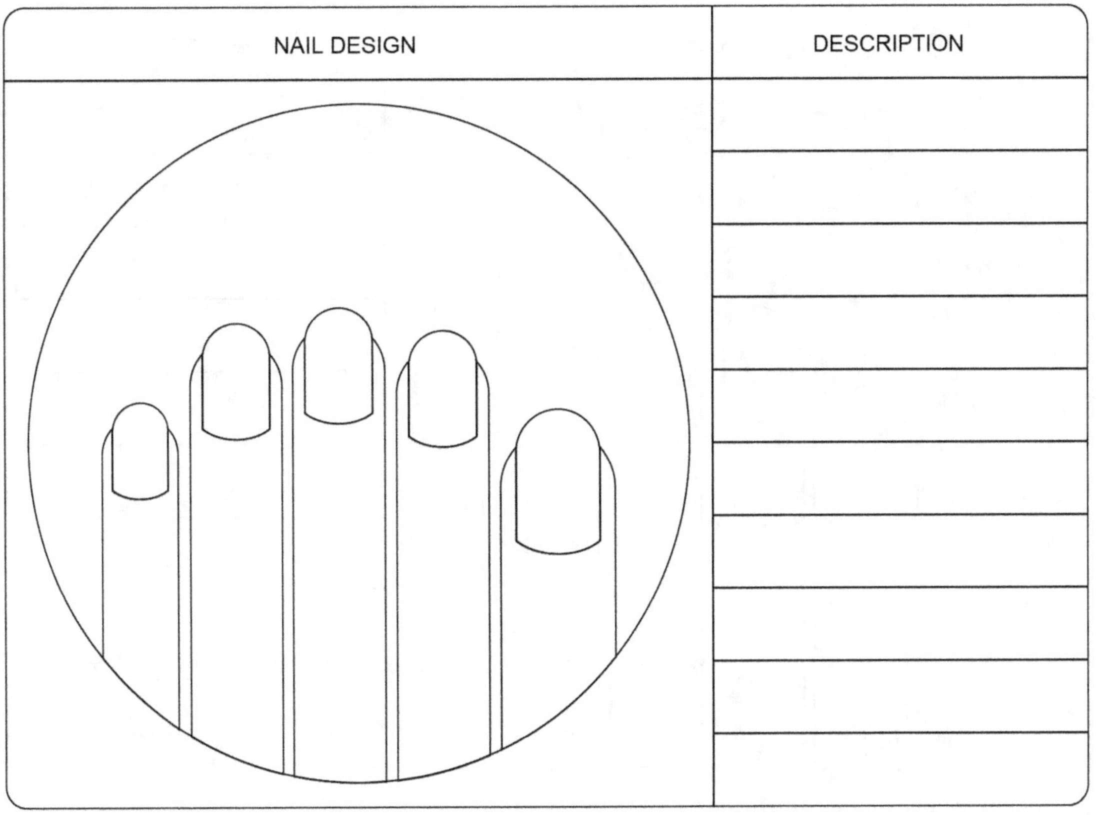	

COLOR PALETTE

1	2	3	4	5	6	7	8

NR	COLOR	BRAND
1		
2		
3		
4		
5		
6		
7		
8		

DETAILS & PATTERNS

ADDITIONAL NOTES

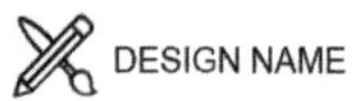 DESIGN NAME ....

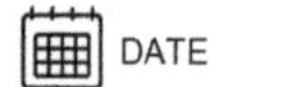 DATE ....

NAIL DESIGN	DESCRIPTION
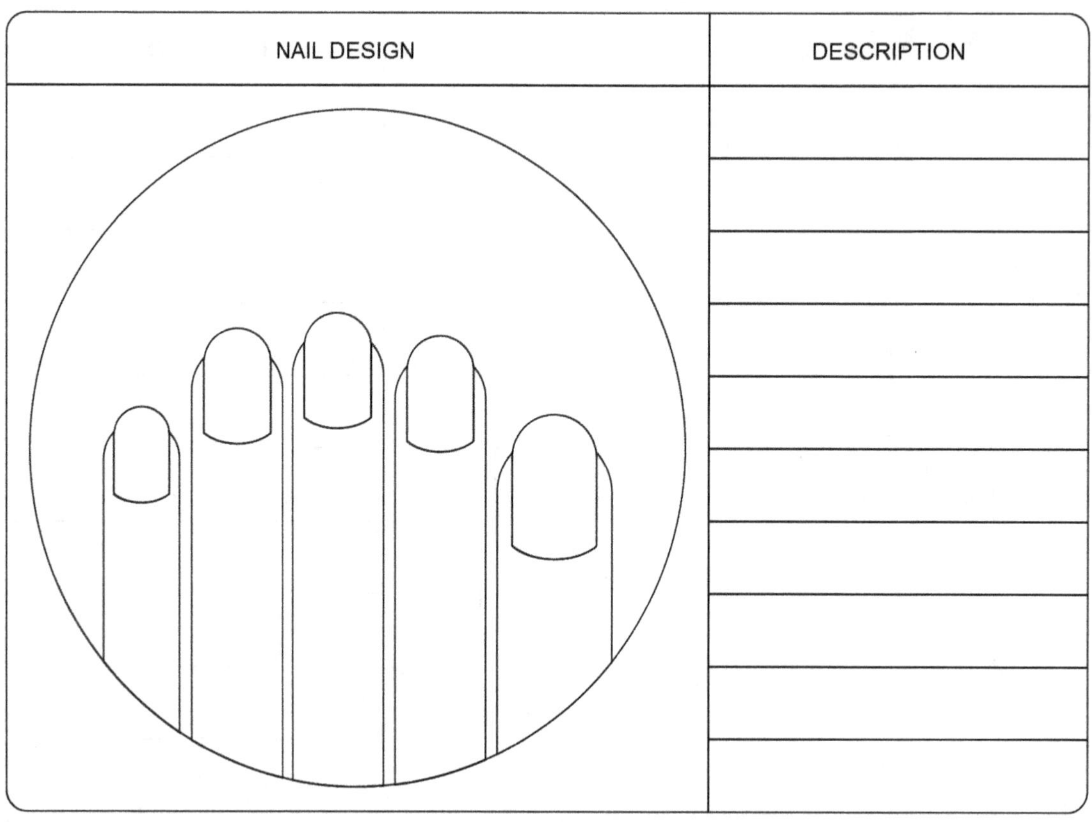	

COLOR PALETTE

1	2	3	4	5	6	7	8

NR	COLOR	BRAND
1		
2		
3		
4		
5		
6		
7		
8		

DETAILS & PATTERNS

ADDITIONAL NOTES

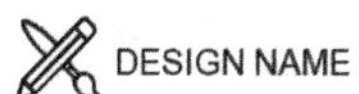

DESIGN NAME .... DATE ....

NAIL DESIGN	DESCRIPTION
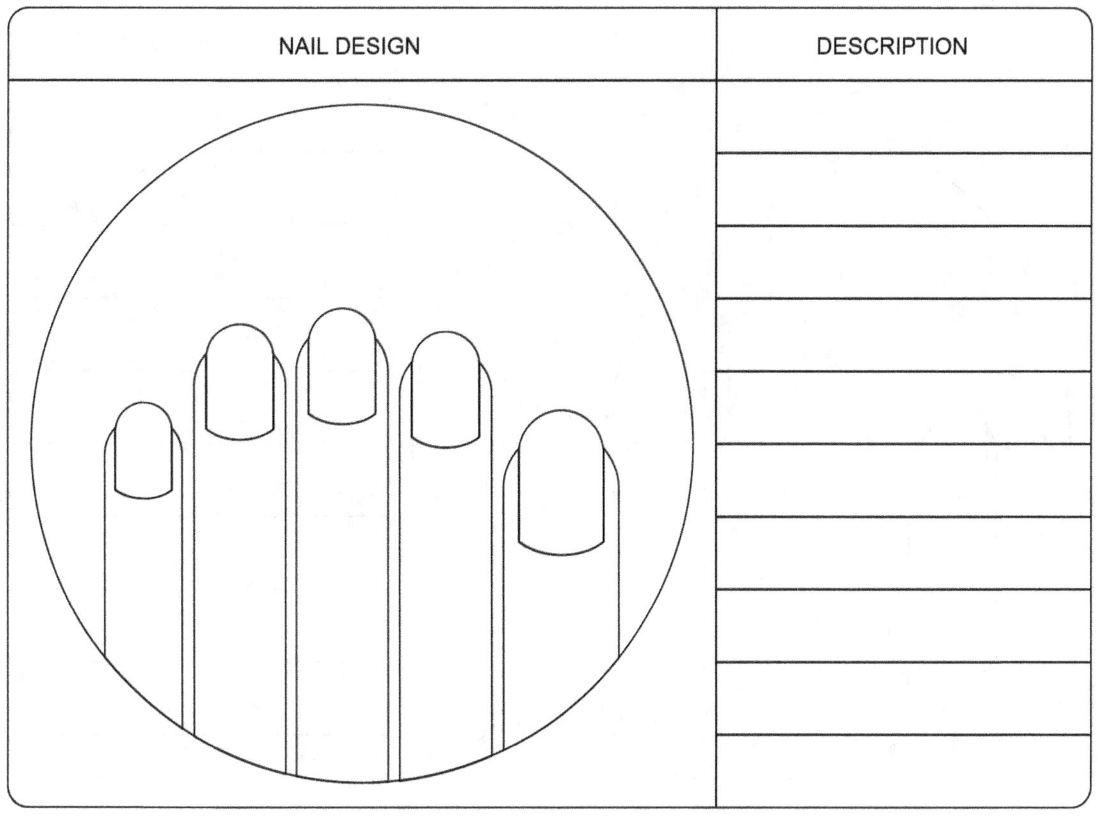	

COLOR PALETTE

1	2	3	4	5	6	7	8

NR	COLOR	BRAND
1		
2		
3		
4		
5		
6		
7		
8		

DETAILS & PATTERNS

ADDITIONAL NOTES

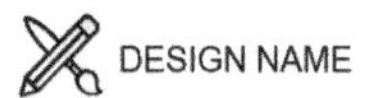

DESIGN NAME ....

DATE ....

NAIL DESIGN	DESCRIPTION
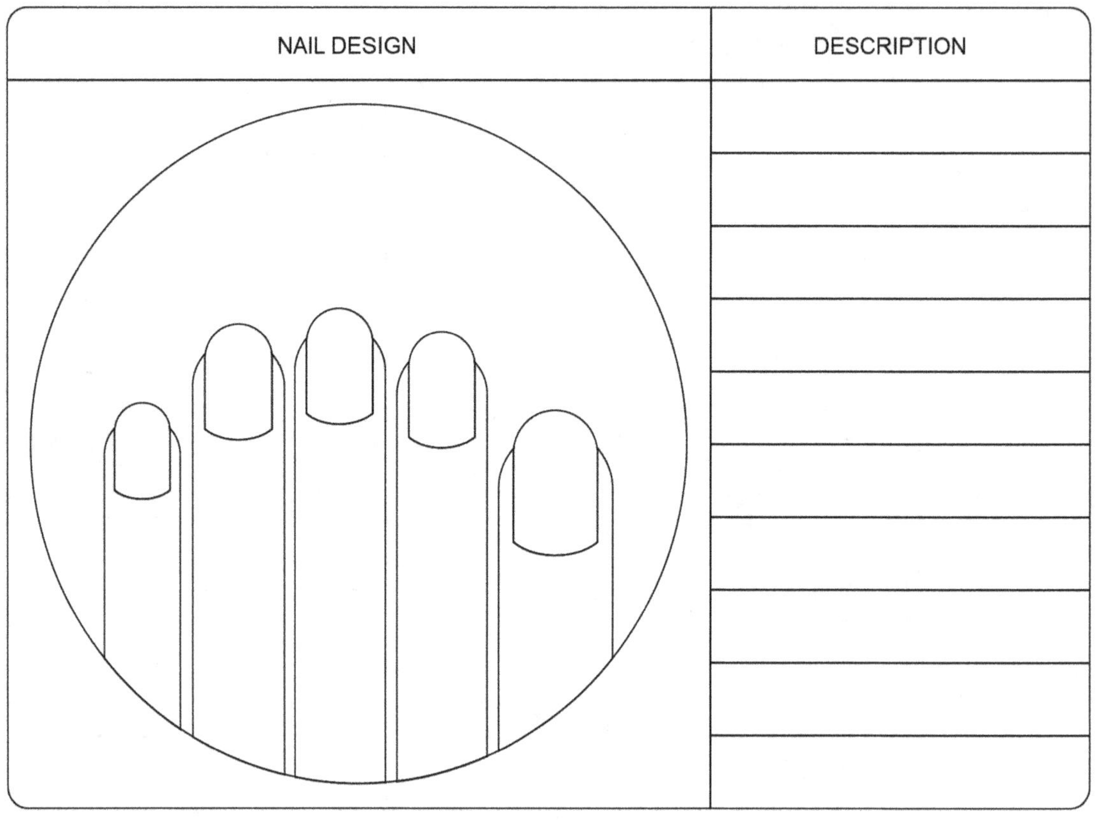	

COLOR PALETTE

1	2	3	4	5	6	7	8

NR	COLOR	BRAND
1		
2		
3		
4		
5		
6		
7		
8		

DETAILS & PATTERNS

ADDITIONAL NOTES

DESIGN NAME .... DATE ....

NAIL DESIGN	DESCRIPTION
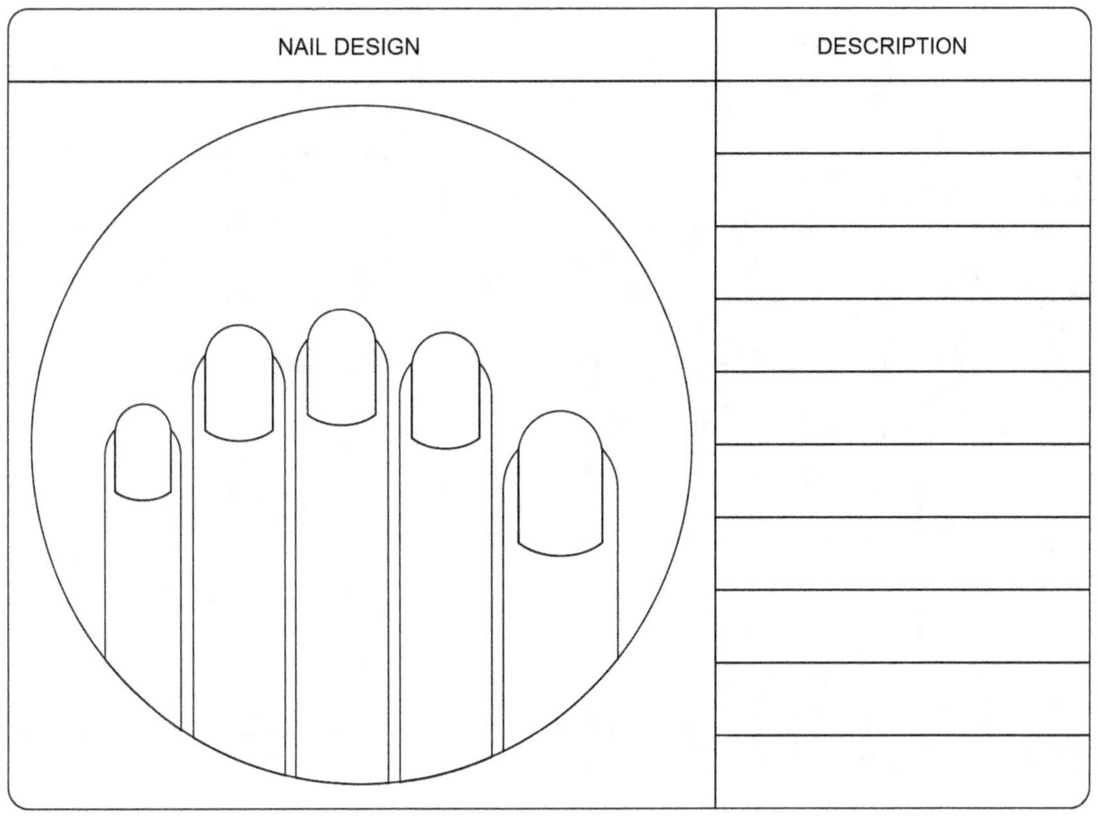	

COLOR PALETTE

1	2	3	4	5	6	7	8

NR	COLOR	BRAND
1		
2		
3		
4		
5		
6		
7		
8		

DETAILS & PATTERNS

ADDITIONAL NOTES

DESIGN NAME .... DATE ....

NAIL DESIGN	DESCRIPTION
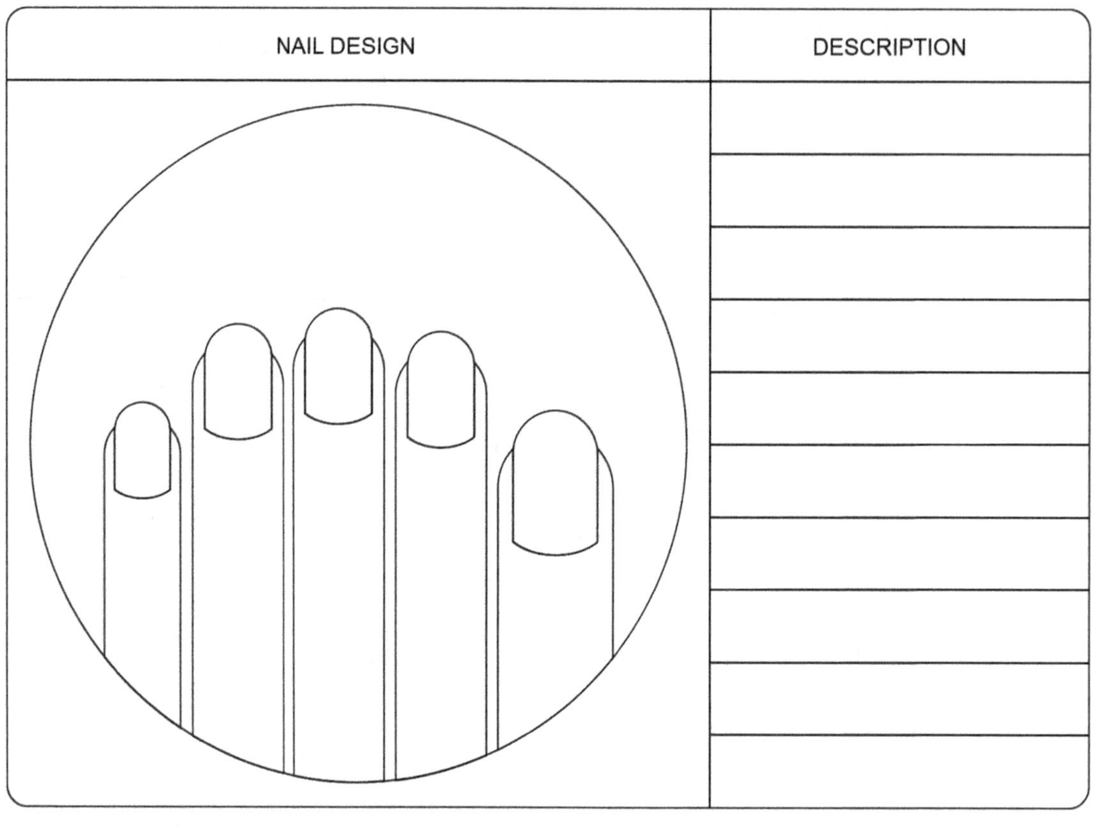	

COLOR PALETTE

1	2	3	4	5	6	7	8

NR	COLOR	BRAND
1		
2		
3		
4		
5		
6		
7		
8		

DETAILS & PATTERNS

ADDITIONAL NOTES

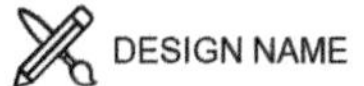
DESIGN NAME ....

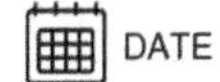
DATE ....

NAIL DESIGN	DESCRIPTION

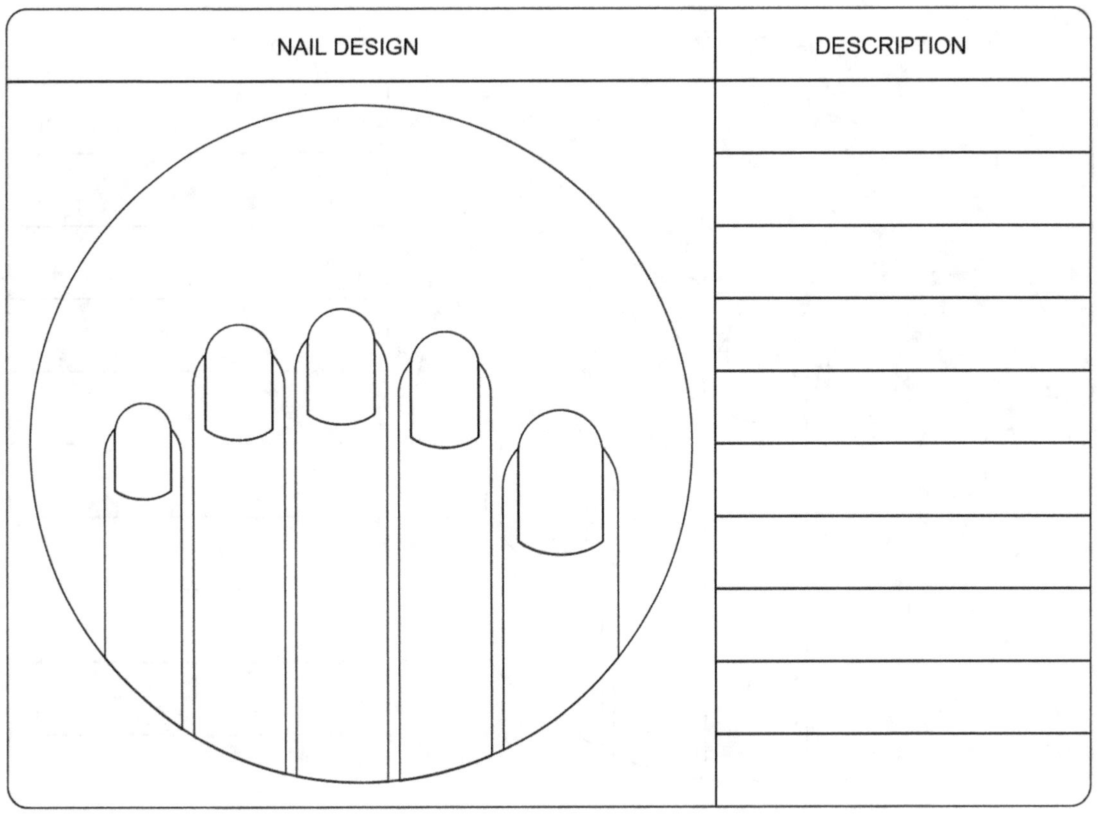

COLOR PALETTE

1	2	3	4	5	6	7	8

NR	COLOR	BRAND
1		
2		
3		
4		
5		
6		
7		
8		

DETAILS & PATTERNS

ADDITIONAL NOTES

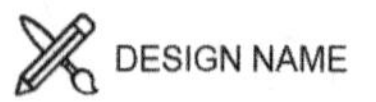 DESIGN NAME .... DATE ....

NAIL DESIGN	DESCRIPTION
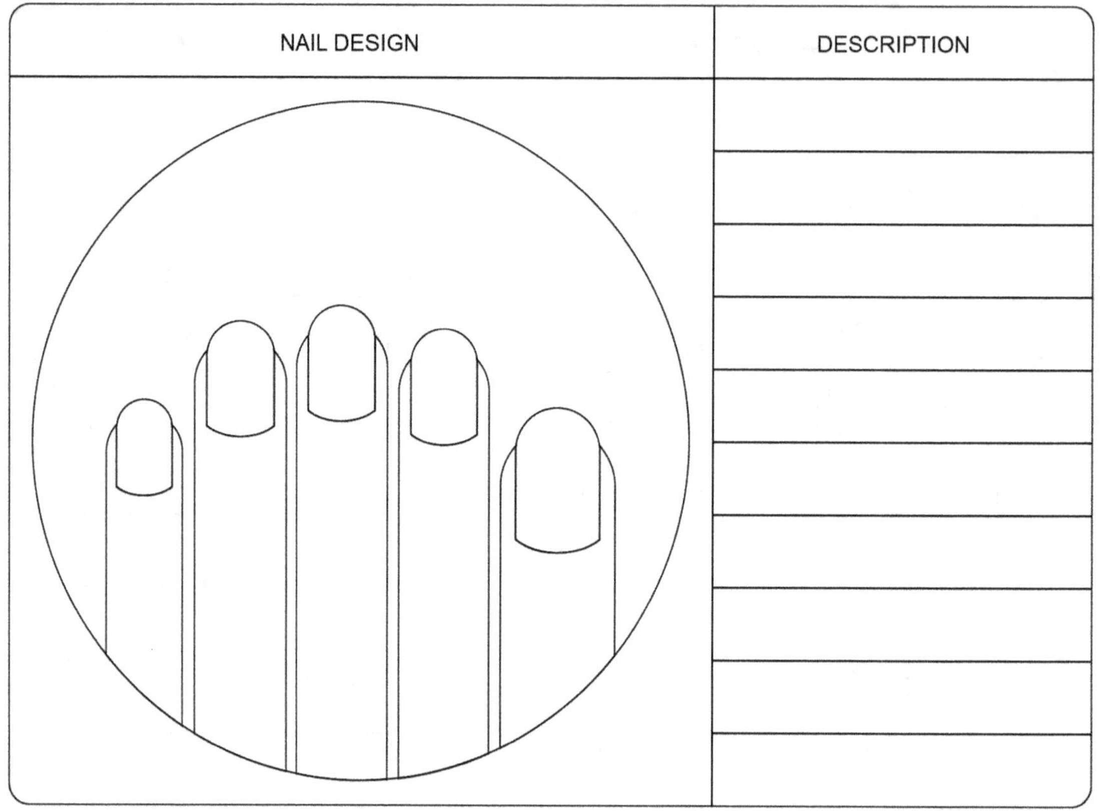	

COLOR PALETTE

1	2	3	4	5	6	7	8

NR	COLOR	BRAND
1		
2		
3		
4		
5		
6		
7		
8		

DETAILS & PATTERNS

ADDITIONAL NOTES

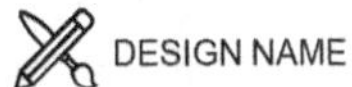

DESIGN NAME ....

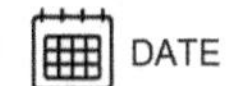

DATE ....

NAIL DESIGN	DESCRIPTION
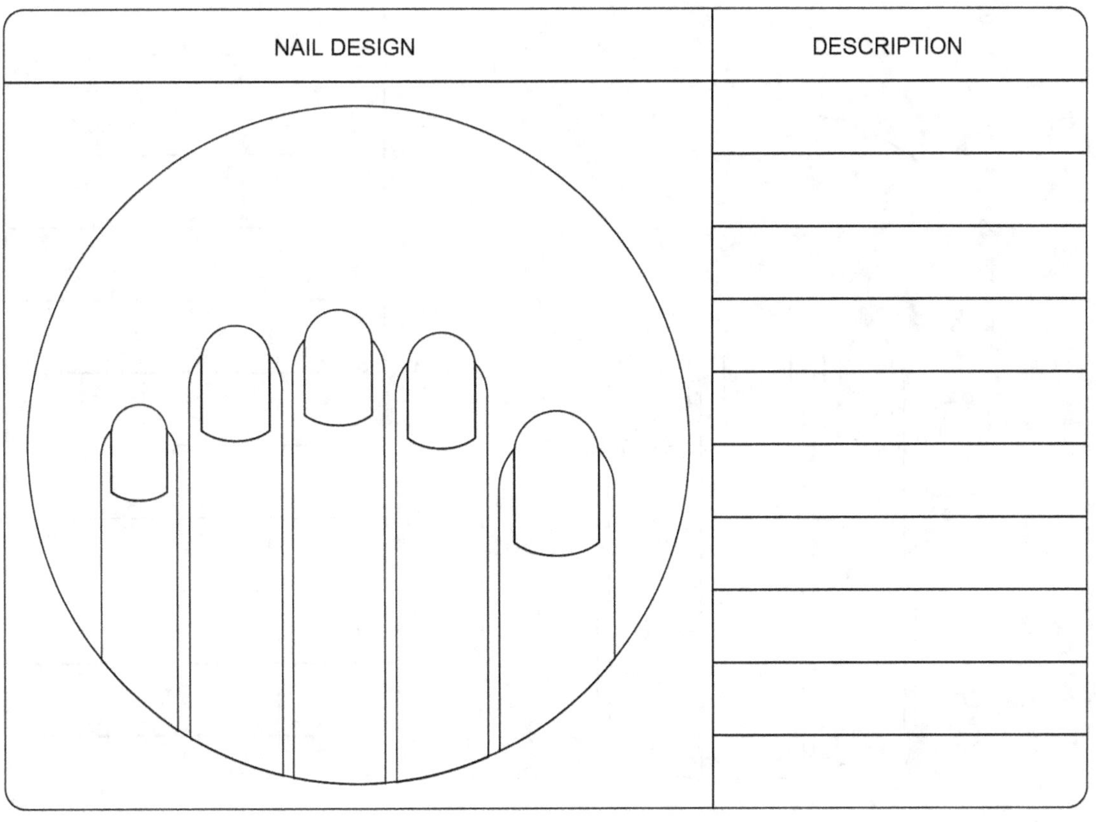	

COLOR PALETTE

1	2	3	4	5	6	7	8

NR	COLOR	BRAND
1		
2		
3		
4		
5		
6		
7		
8		

DETAILS & PATTERNS

ADDITIONAL NOTES

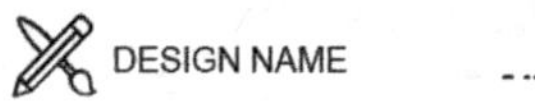

DESIGN NAME ....

DATE ....

NAIL DESIGN	DESCRIPTION
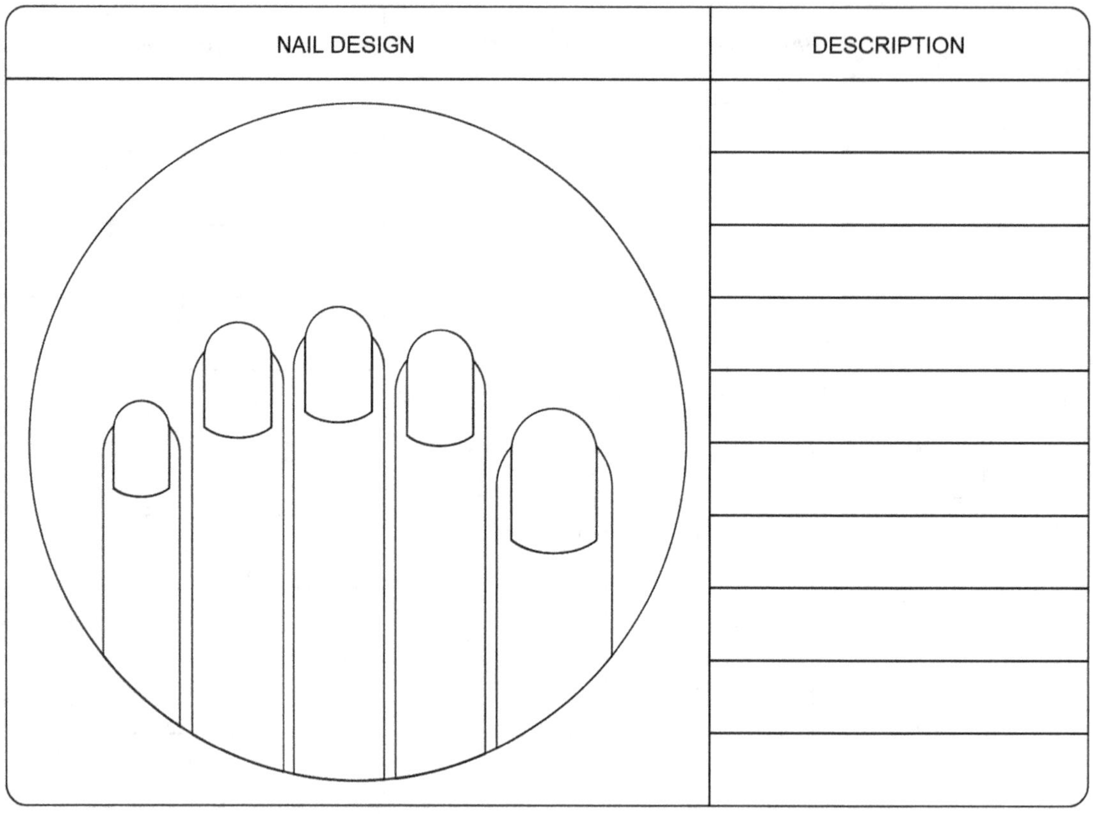	

COLOR PALETTE

1	2	3	4	5	6	7	8

NR	COLOR	BRAND
1		
2		
3		
4		
5		
6		
7		
8		

DETAILS & PATTERNS

ADDITIONAL NOTES

DESIGN NAME .... DATE ....

NAIL DESIGN	DESCRIPTION

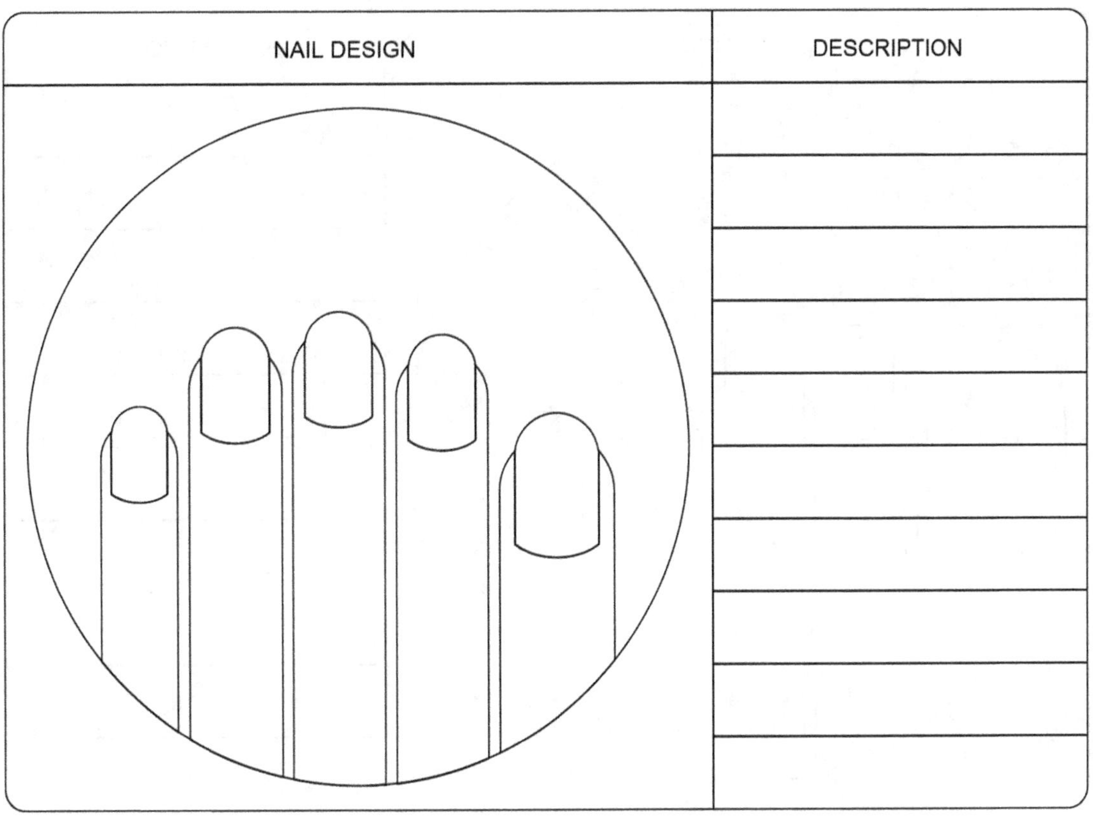

COLOR PALETTE

1	2	3	4	5	6	7	8

NR	COLOR	BRAND
1		
2		
3		
4		
5		
6		
7		
8		

DETAILS & PATTERNS

ADDITIONAL NOTES

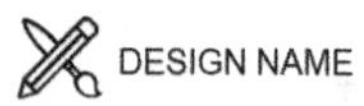 DESIGN NAME ....

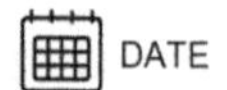 DATE ....

NAIL DESIGN	DESCRIPTION
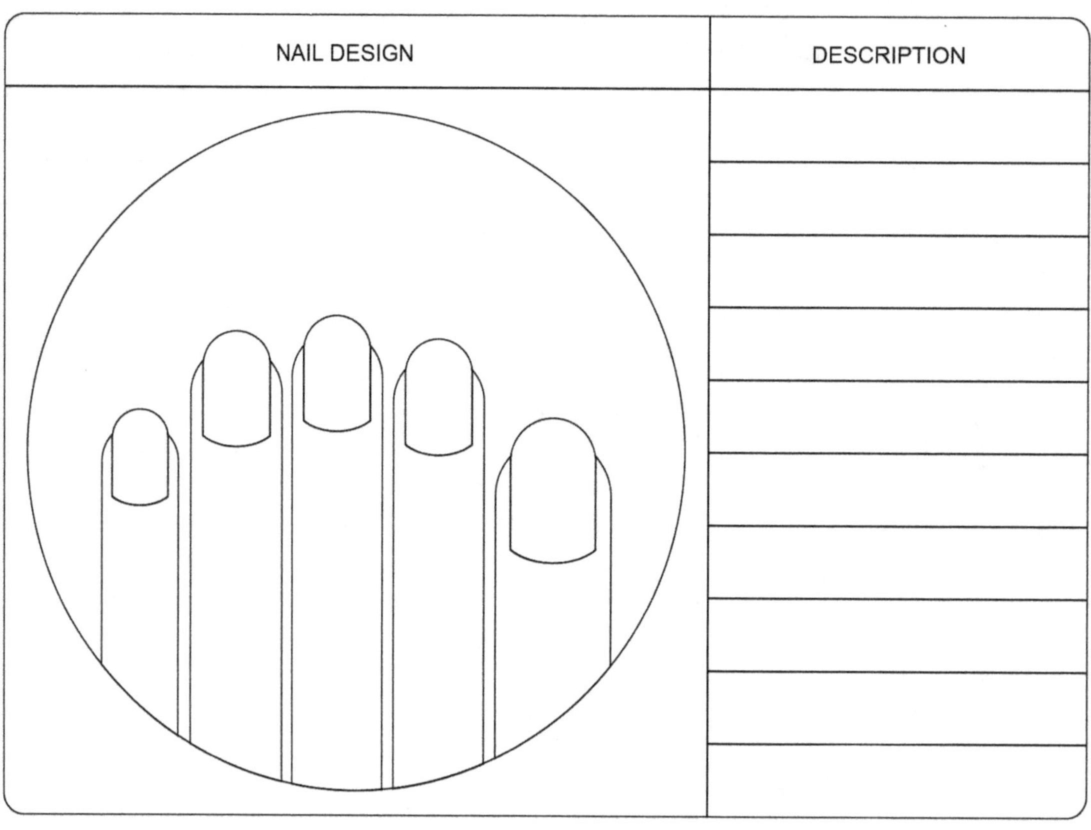	

COLOR PALETTE

1	2	3	4	5	6	7	8

NR	COLOR	BRAND
1		
2		
3		
4		
5		
6		
7		
8		

DETAILS & PATTERNS

ADDITIONAL NOTES

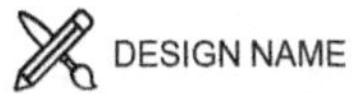
DESIGN NAME ....

DATE ....

NAIL DESIGN	DESCRIPTION

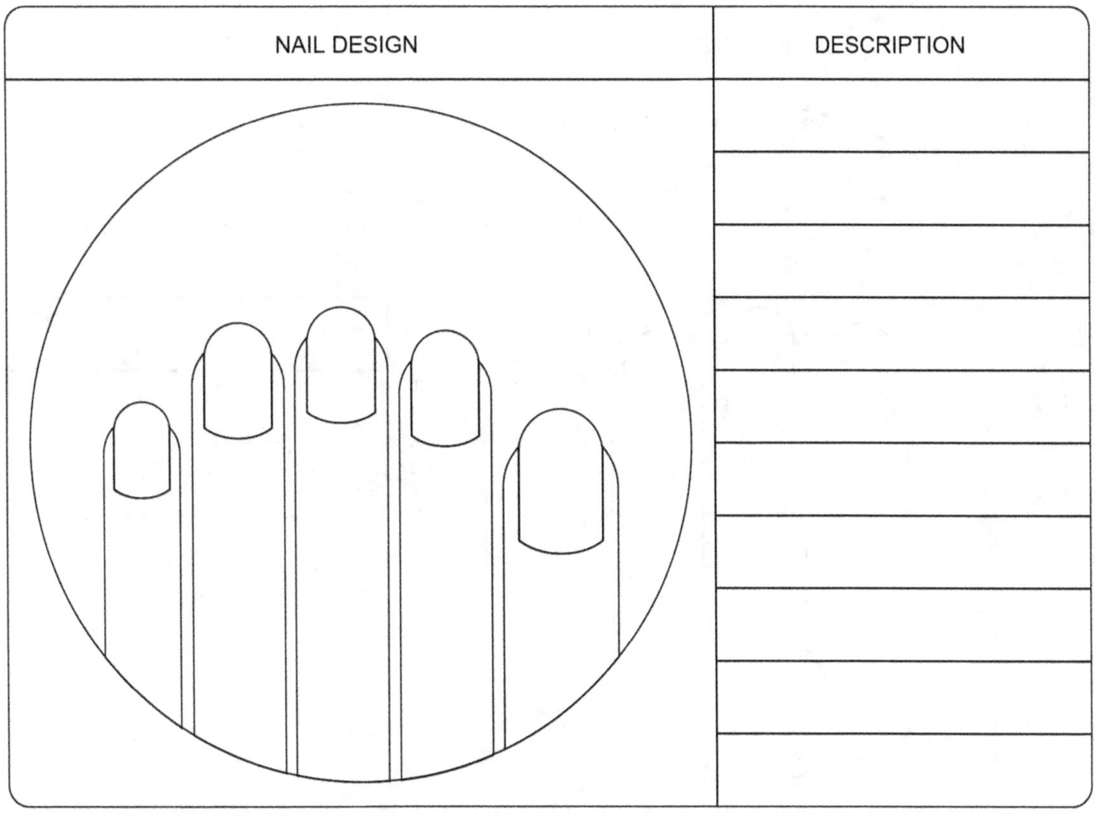

COLOR PALETTE

1	2	3	4	5	6	7	8

NR	COLOR	BRAND
1		
2		
3		
4		
5		
6		
7		
8		

DETAILS & PATTERNS

ADDITIONAL NOTES

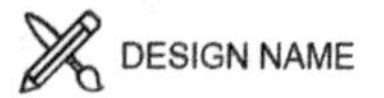

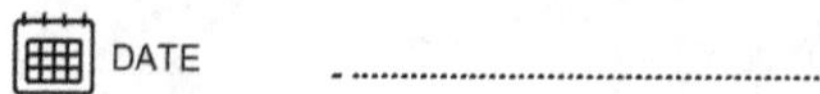

NAIL DESIGN	DESCRIPTION
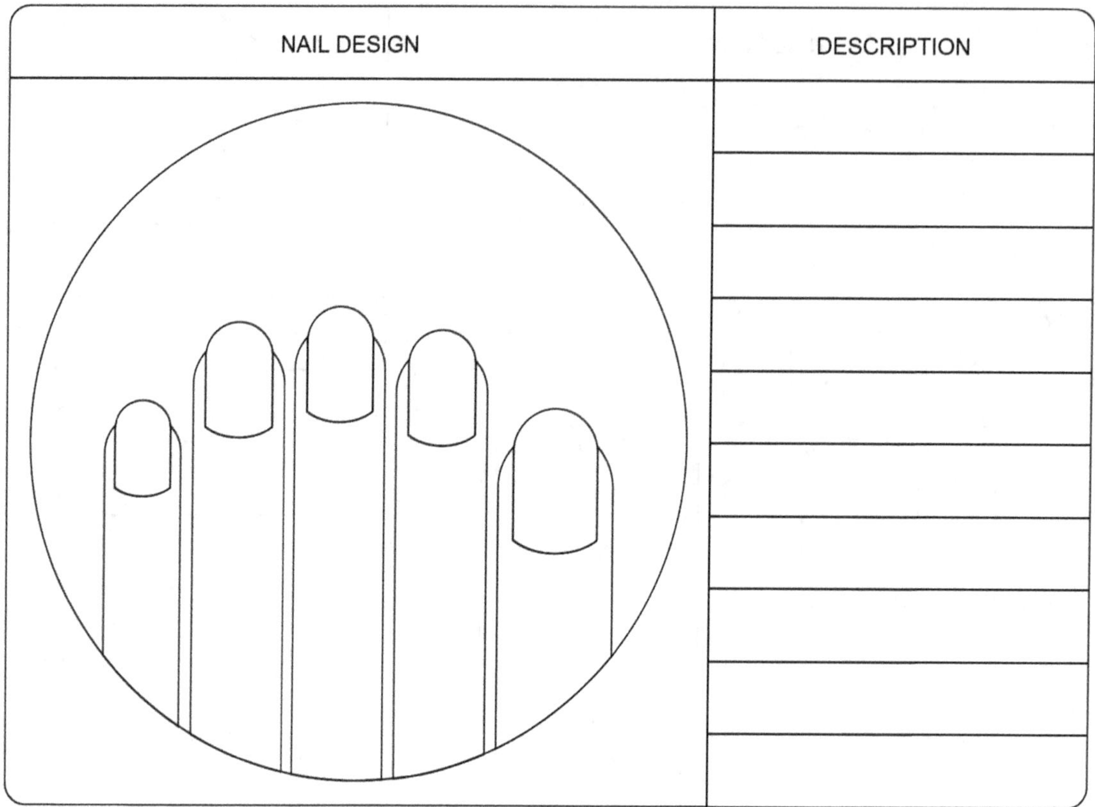	

COLOR PALETTE

1	2	3	4	5	6	7	8

NR	COLOR	BRAND
1		
2		
3		
4		
5		
6		
7		
8		

DETAILS & PATTERNS

ADDITIONAL NOTES

DESIGN NAME .... DATE ....

NAIL DESIGN	DESCRIPTION

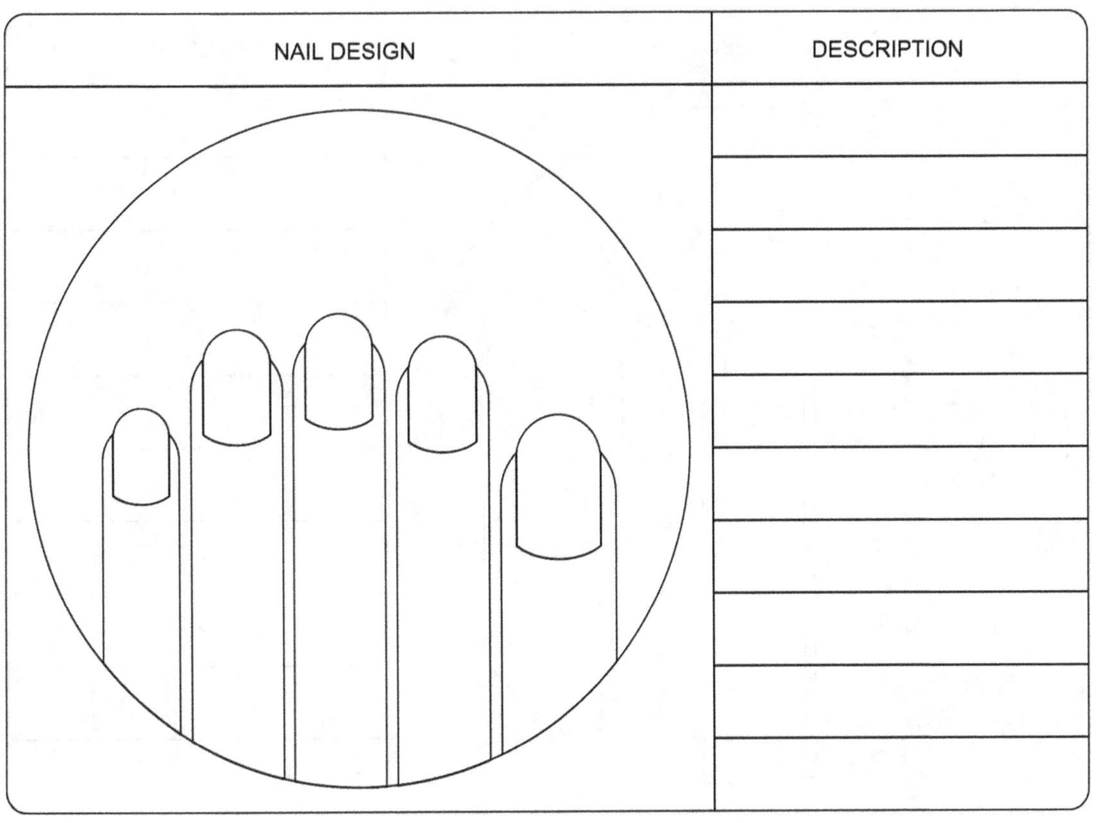

COLOR PALETTE

1	2	3	4	5	6	7	8

NR	COLOR	BRAND
1		
2		
3		
4		
5		
6		
7		
8		

DETAILS & PATTERNS

ADDITIONAL NOTES

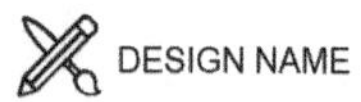 DESIGN NAME ....

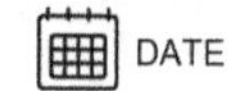 DATE ....

NAIL DESIGN	DESCRIPTION
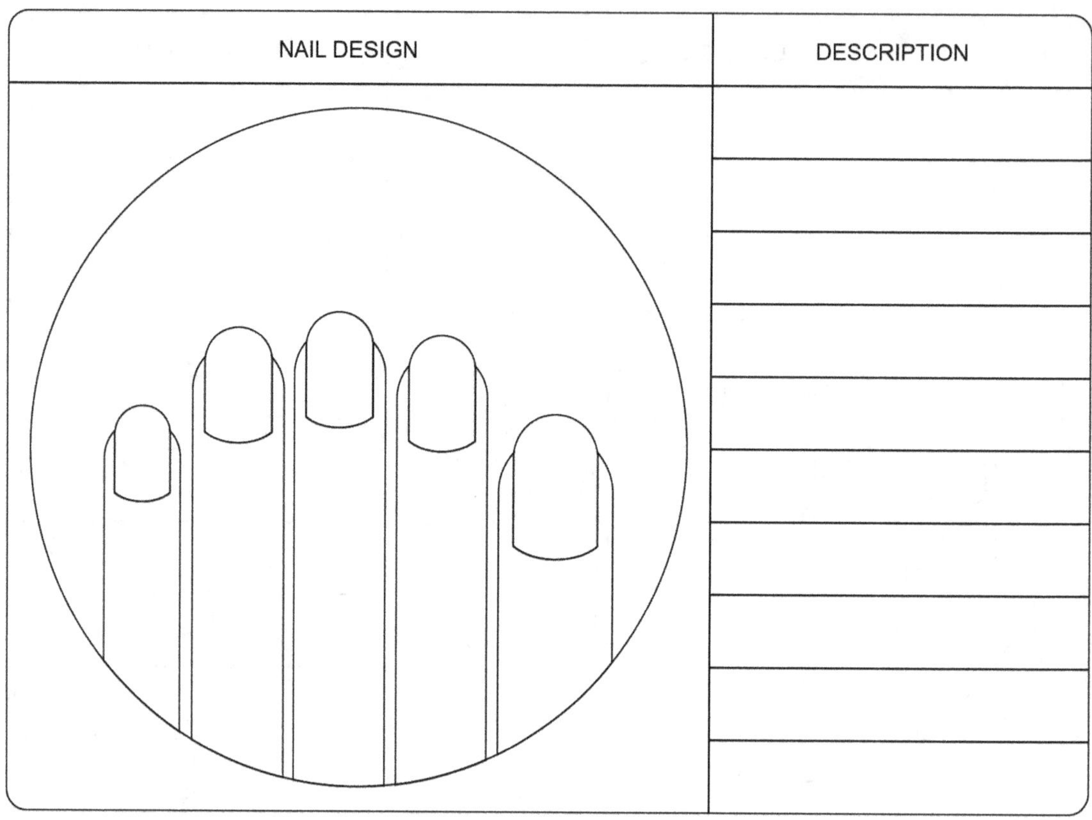	

COLOR PALETTE

1	2	3	4	5	6	7	8

NR	COLOR	BRAND
1		
2		
3		
4		
5		
6		
7		
8		

DETAILS & PATTERNS

ADDITIONAL NOTES

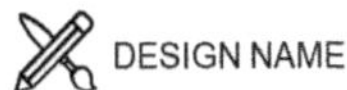
DESIGN NAME ....

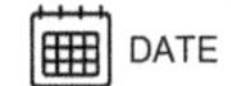
DATE ....

NAIL DESIGN	DESCRIPTION
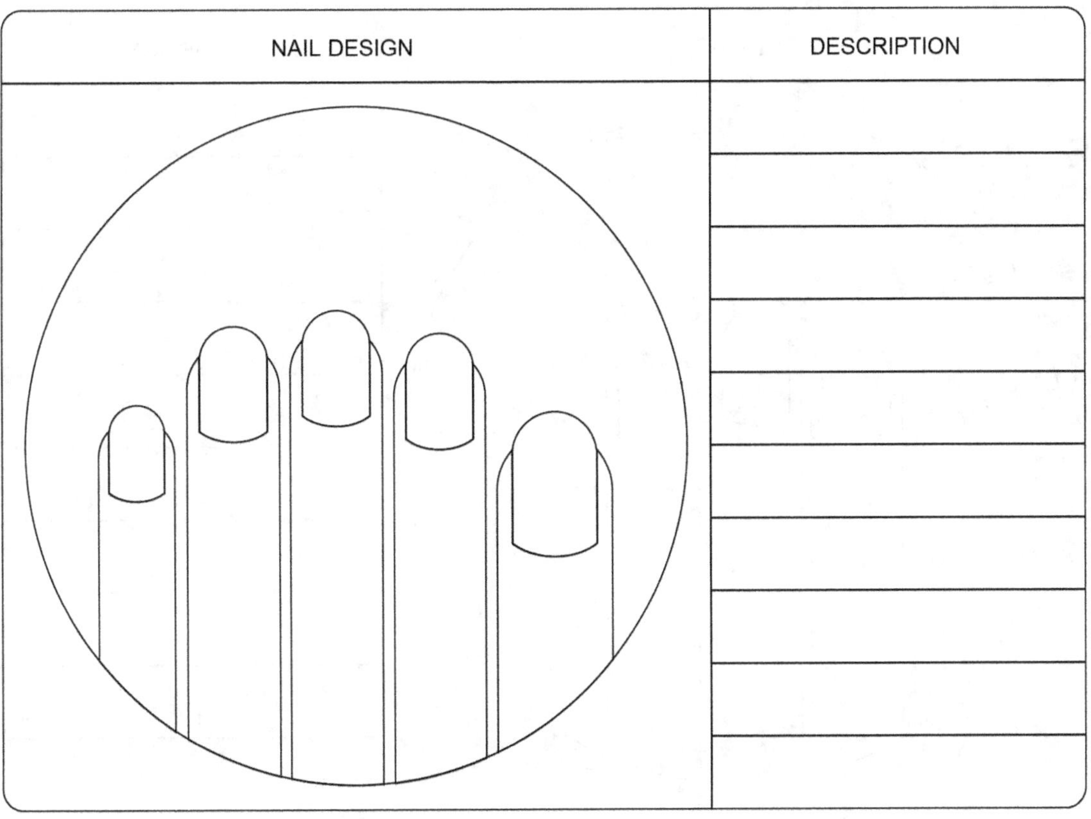	

COLOR PALETTE

1	2	3	4	5	6	7	8

NR	COLOR	BRAND
1		
2		
3		
4		
5		
6		
7		
8		

DETAILS & PATTERNS

ADDITIONAL NOTES

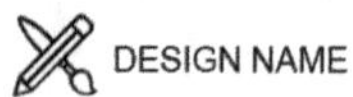
DESIGN NAME ....

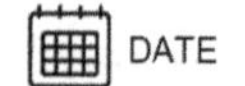
DATE ....

NAIL DESIGN	DESCRIPTION
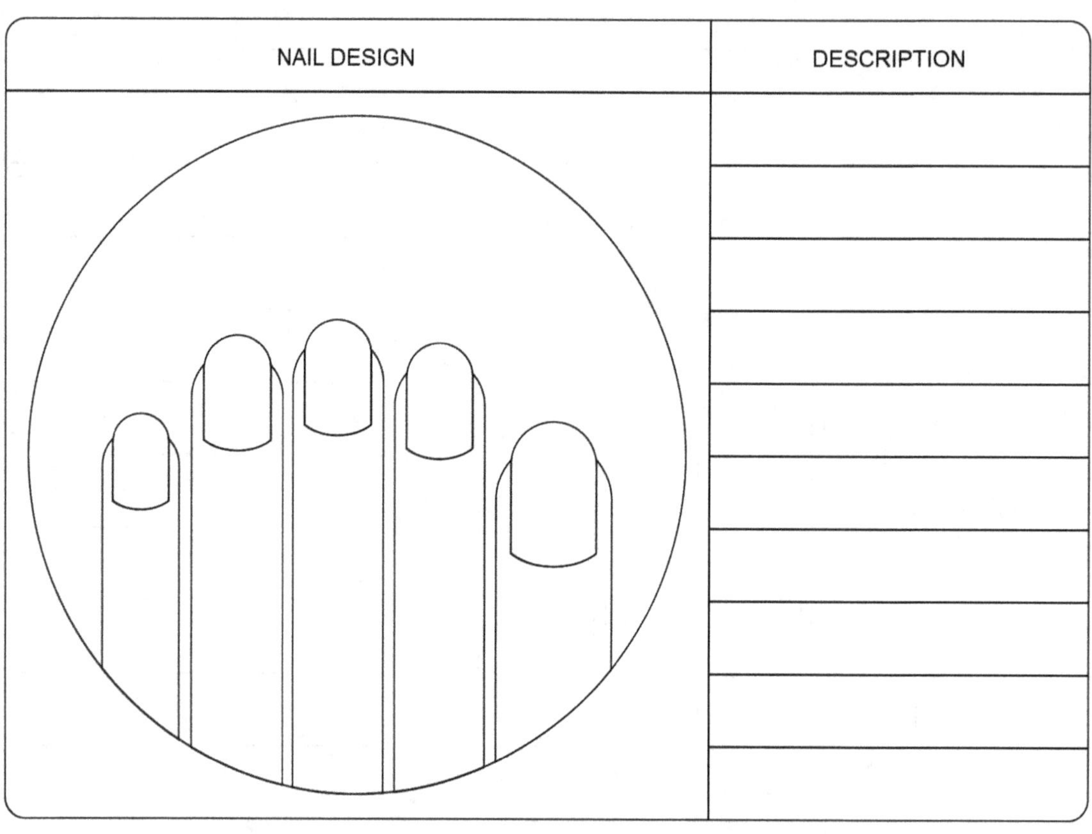	

COLOR PALETTE

1	2	3	4	5	6	7	8

NR	COLOR	BRAND
1		
2		
3		
4		
5		
6		
7		
8		

DETAILS & PATTERNS

ADDITIONAL NOTES

DESIGN NAME .... DATE ....

NAIL DESIGN	DESCRIPTION
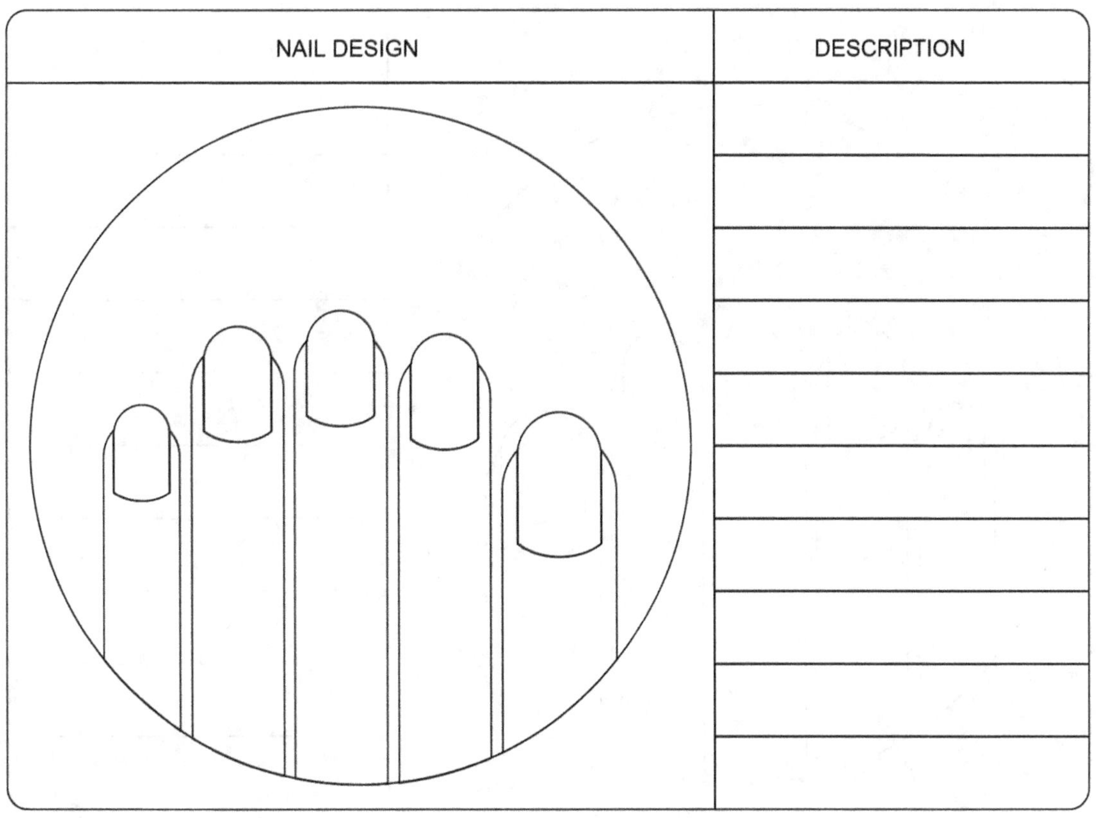	

COLOR PALETTE

1	2	3	4	5	6	7	8

NR	COLOR	BRAND
1		
2		
3		
4		
5		
6		
7		
8		

DETAILS & PATTERNS

ADDITIONAL NOTES

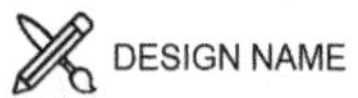 DESIGN NAME ....

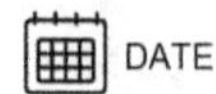 DATE ....

NAIL DESIGN	DESCRIPTION
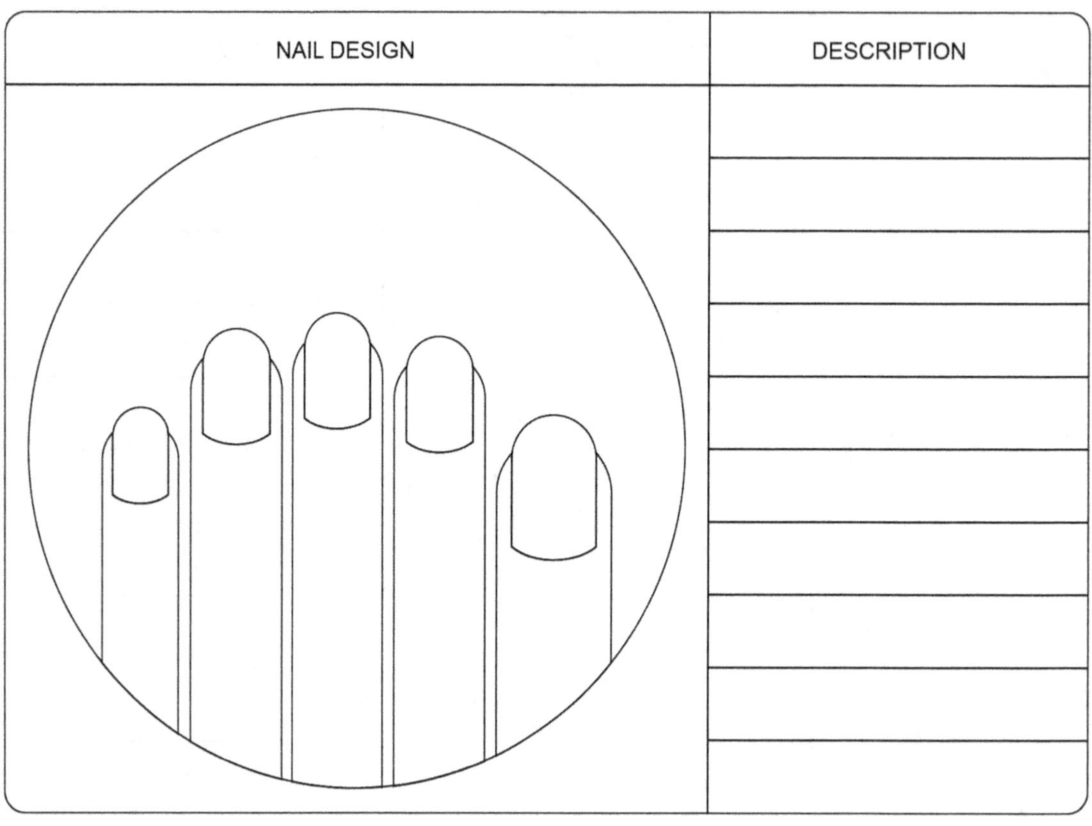	

COLOR PALETTE

1	2	3	4	5	6	7	8

NR	COLOR	BRAND
1		
2		
3		
4		
5		
6		
7		
8		

DETAILS & PATTERNS

ADDITIONAL NOTES

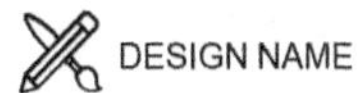 DESIGN NAME .... 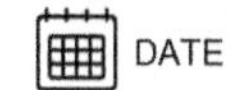 DATE ....

NAIL DESIGN	DESCRIPTION
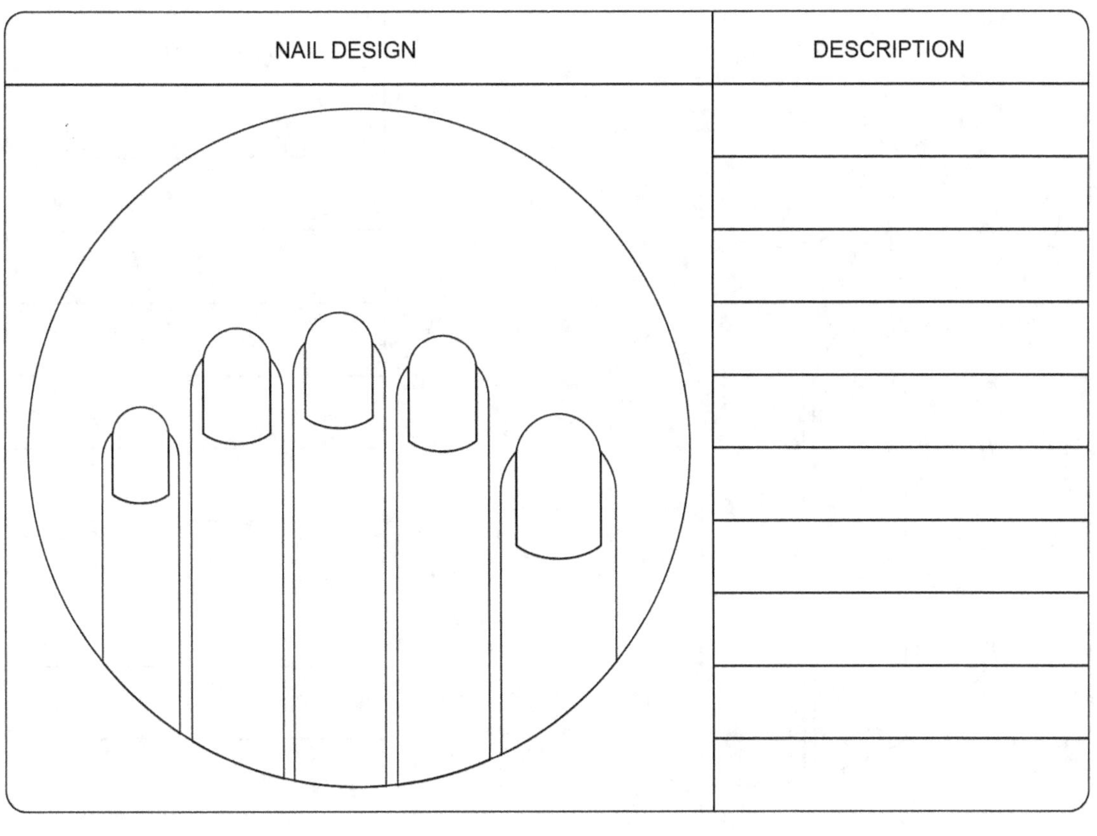	

COLOR PALETTE							
1	2	3	4	5	6	7	8

NR	COLOR	BRAND
1		
2		
3		
4		
5		
6		
7		
8		

DETAILS & PATTERNS

ADDITIONAL NOTES

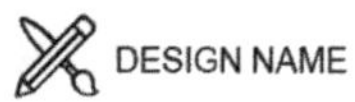

DESIGN NAME ....

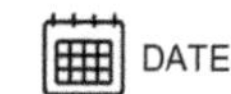

DATE ....

NAIL DESIGN	DESCRIPTION

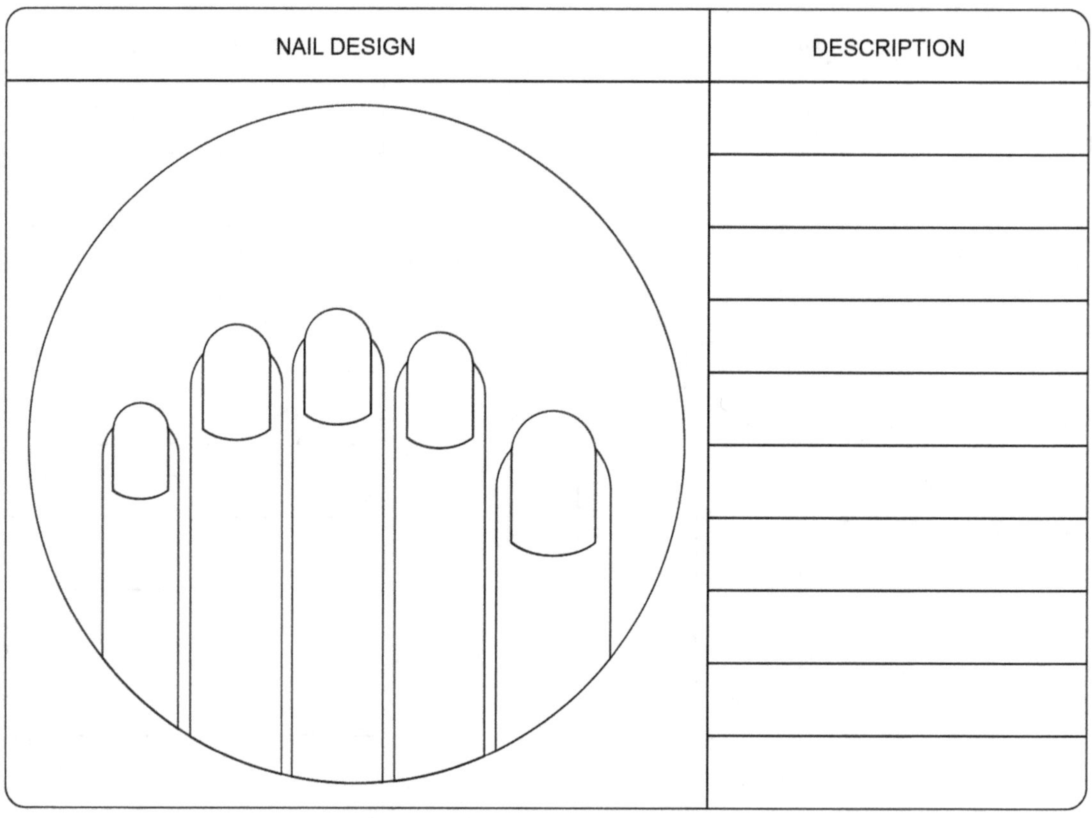

COLOR PALETTE

1	2	3	4	5	6	7	8

NR	COLOR	BRAND
1		
2		
3		
4		
5		
6		
7		
8		

DETAILS & PATTERNS

ADDITIONAL NOTES

DESIGN NAME .... DATE ....

NAIL DESIGN	DESCRIPTION
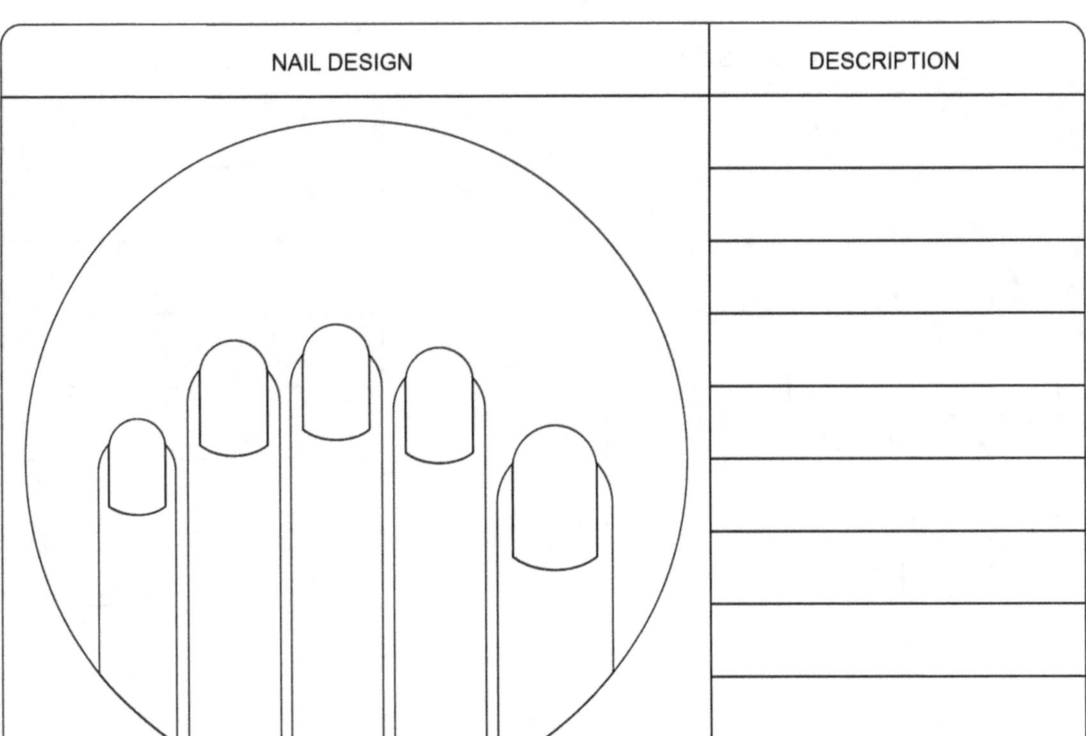	

COLOR PALETTE

1	2	3	4	5	6	7	8

NR	COLOR	BRAND
1		
2		
3		
4		
5		
6		
7		
8		

DETAILS & PATTERNS

ADDITIONAL NOTES

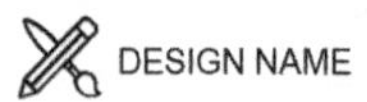 DESIGN NAME 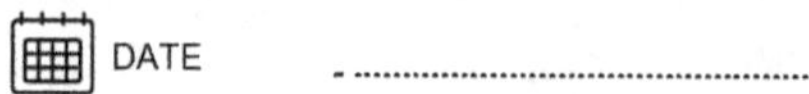 DATE

NAIL DESIGN	DESCRIPTION

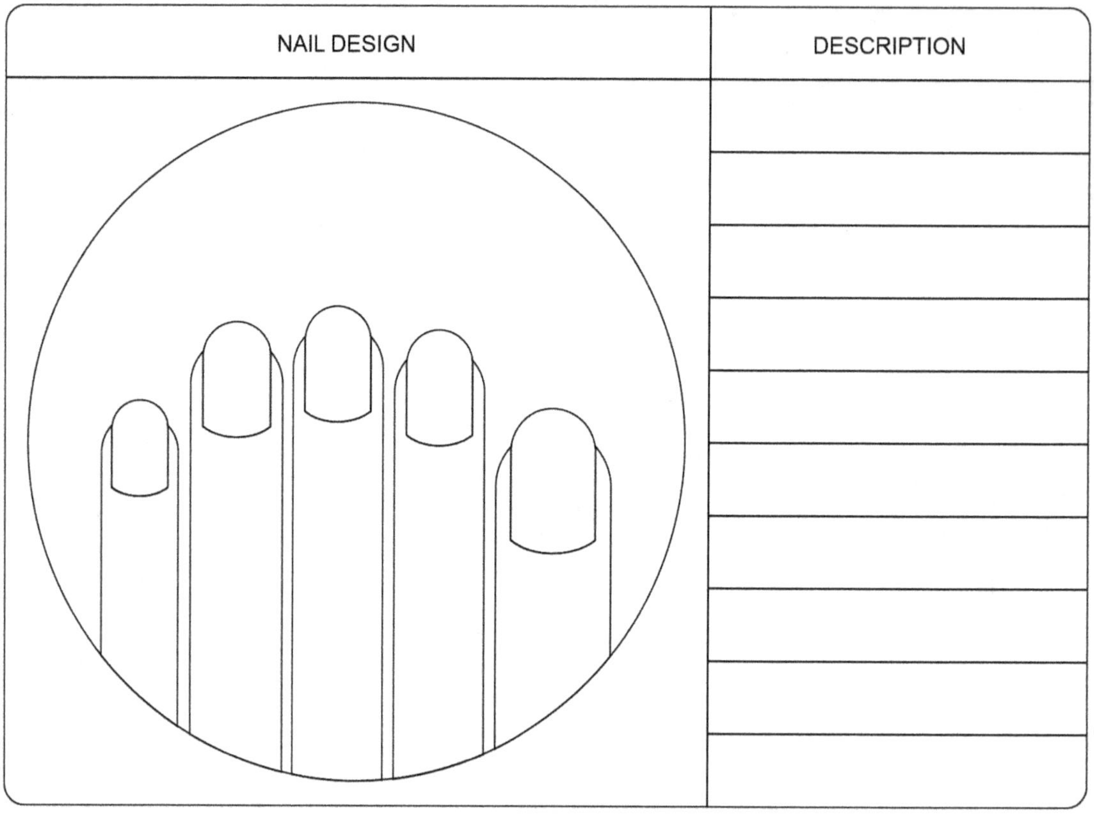

COLOR PALETTE

1	2	3	4	5	6	7	8

NR	COLOR	BRAND
1		
2		
3		
4		
5		
6		
7		
8		

DETAILS & PATTERNS

ADDITIONAL NOTES

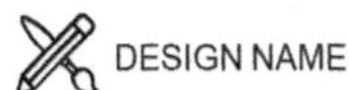 DESIGN NAME ....

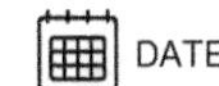 DATE ....

NAIL DESIGN	DESCRIPTION
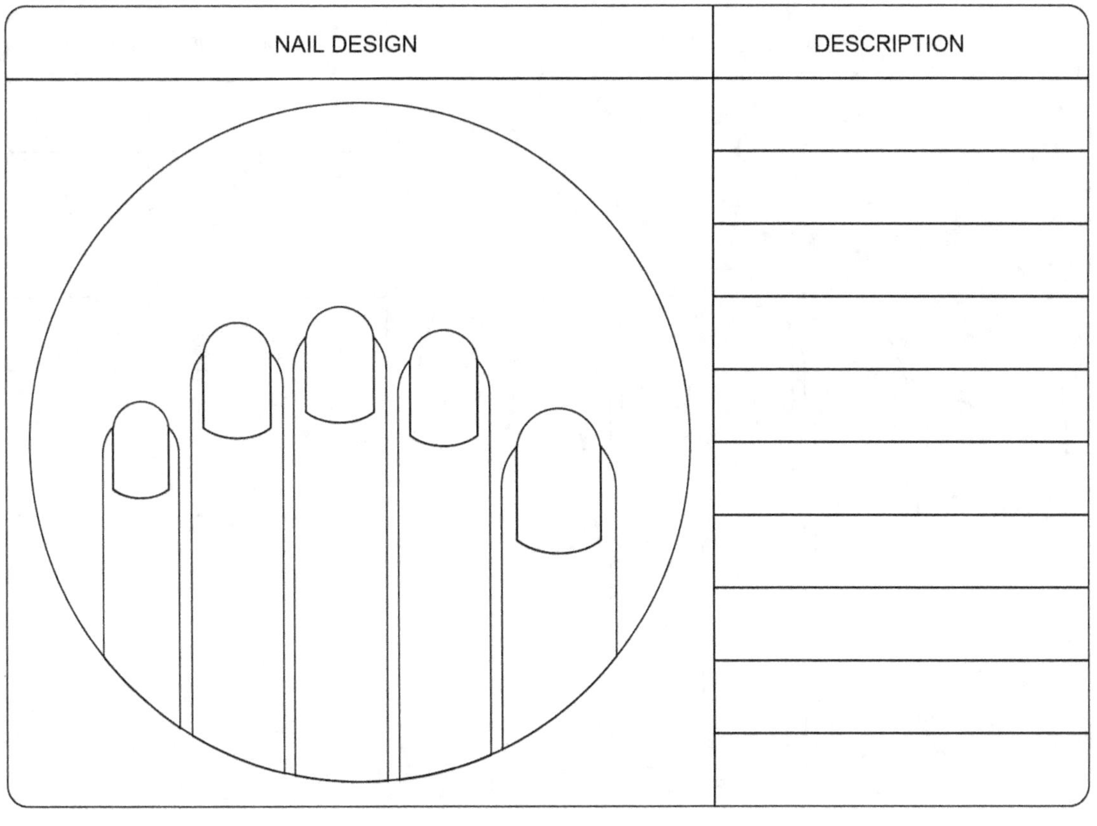	

COLOR PALETTE

1	2	3	4	5	6	7	8

NR	COLOR	BRAND
1		
2		
3		
4		
5		
6		
7		
8		

DETAILS & PATTERNS

ADDITIONAL NOTES

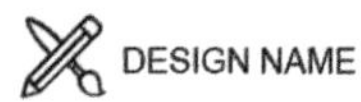 DESIGN NAME ....

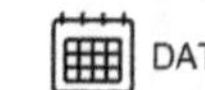 DATE ....

NAIL DESIGN	DESCRIPTION
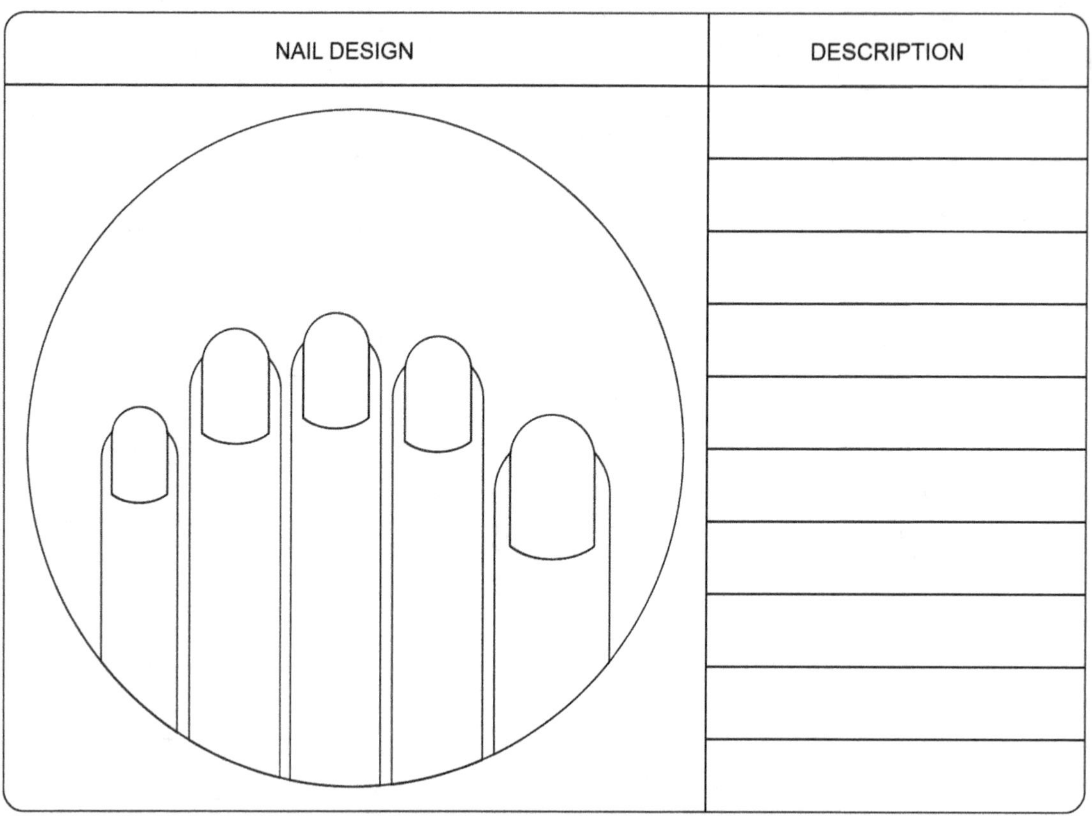	

COLOR PALETTE

1	2	3	4	5	6	7	8

NR	COLOR	BRAND
1		
2		
3		
4		
5		
6		
7		
8		

DETAILS & PATTERNS

ADDITIONAL NOTES

DESIGN NAME .... DATE ....

NAIL DESIGN	DESCRIPTION
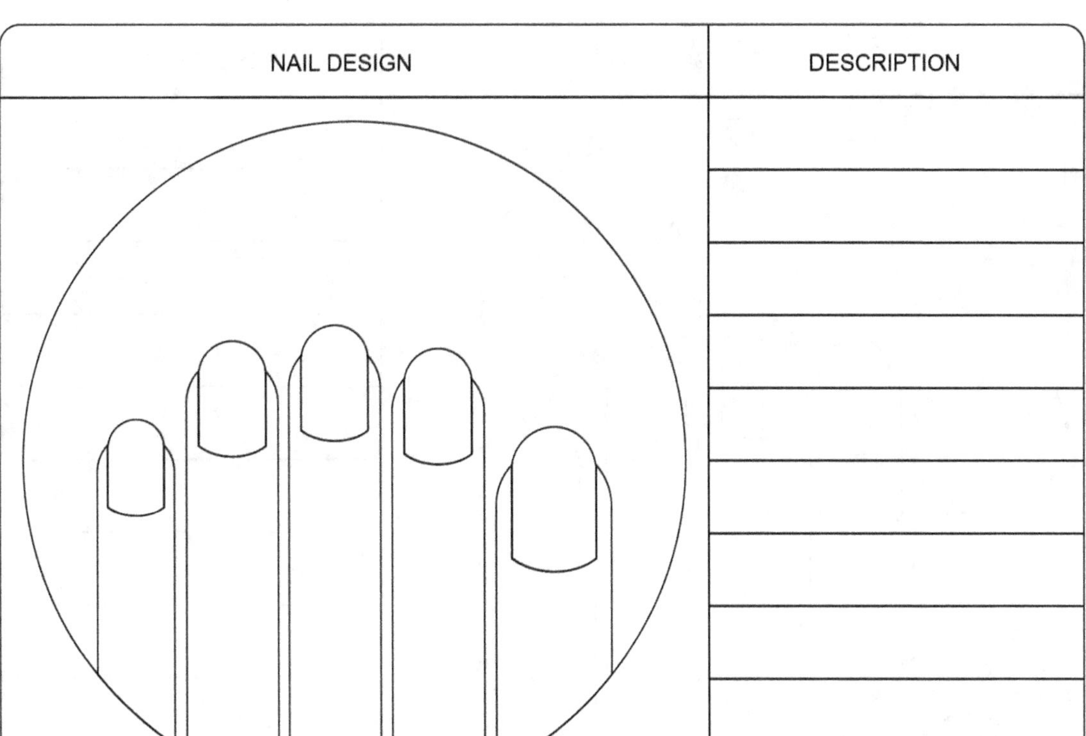	

COLOR PALETTE

1	2	3	4	5	6	7	8

NR	COLOR	BRAND
1		
2		
3		
4		
5		
6		
7		
8		

DETAILS & PATTERNS

ADDITIONAL NOTES

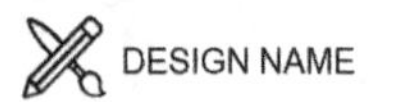

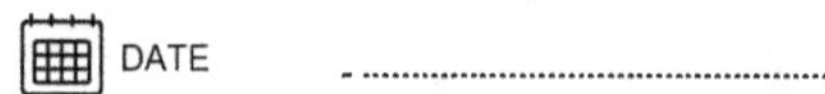

NAIL DESIGN	DESCRIPTION
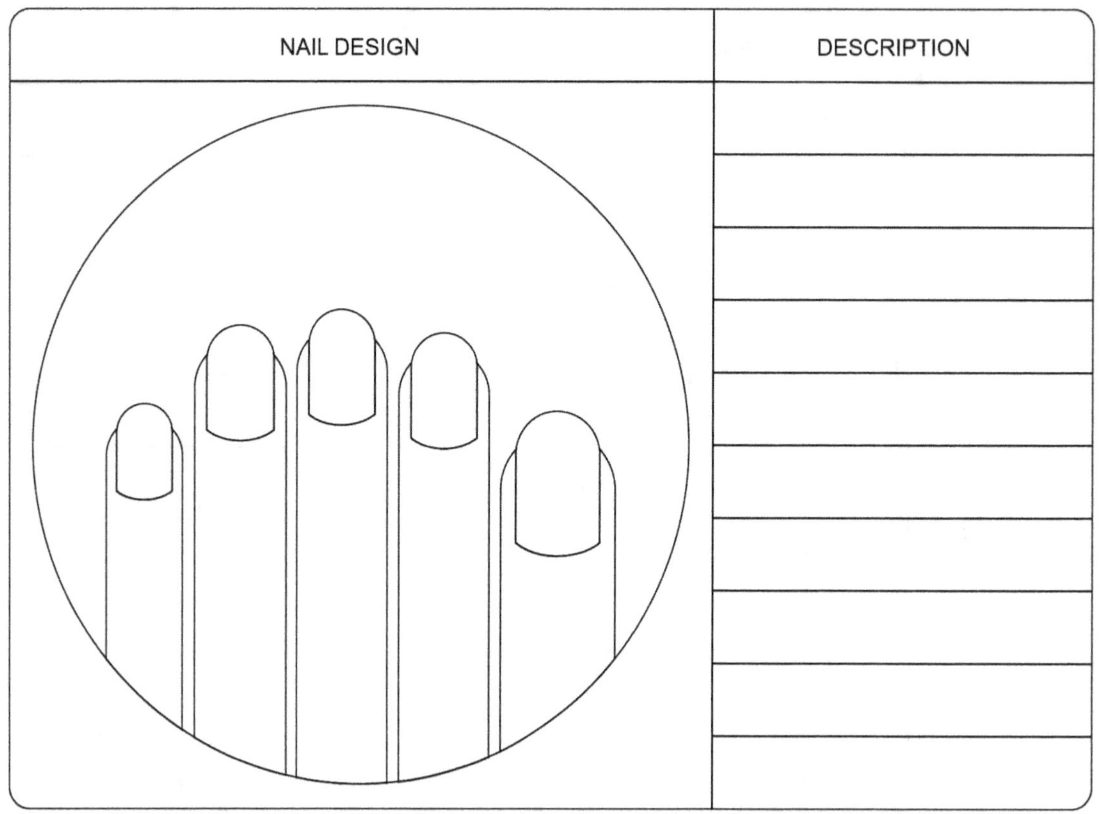	

COLOR PALETTE

1	2	3	4	5	6	7	8

NR	COLOR	BRAND
1		
2		
3		
4		
5		
6		
7		
8		

DETAILS & PATTERNS

ADDITIONAL NOTES

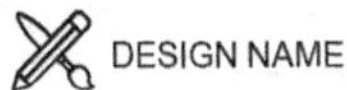

DESIGN NAME .... DATE ....

NAIL DESIGN	DESCRIPTION
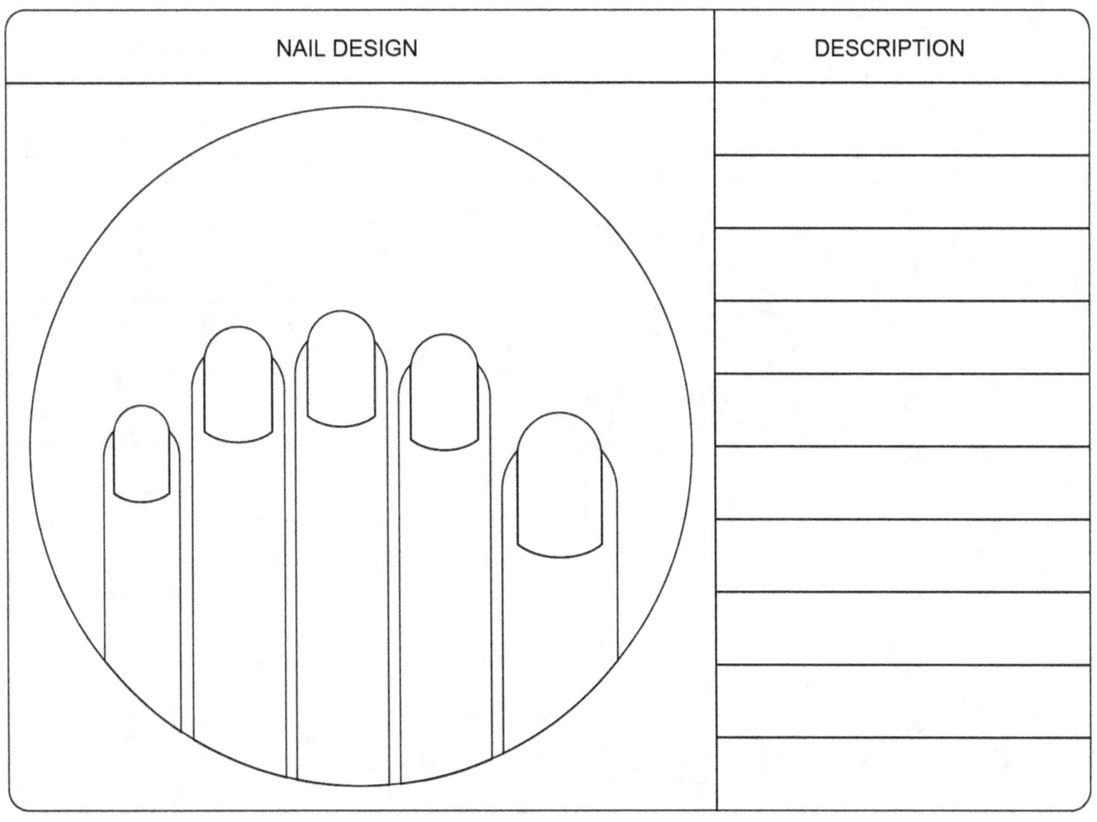	

COLOR PALETTE

1	2	3	4	5	6	7	8

NR	COLOR	BRAND
1		
2		
3		
4		
5		
6		
7		
8		

DETAILS & PATTERNS

ADDITIONAL NOTES

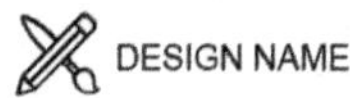 DESIGN NAME ....

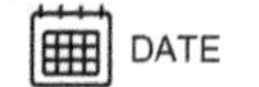 DATE ....

NAIL DESIGN	DESCRIPTION
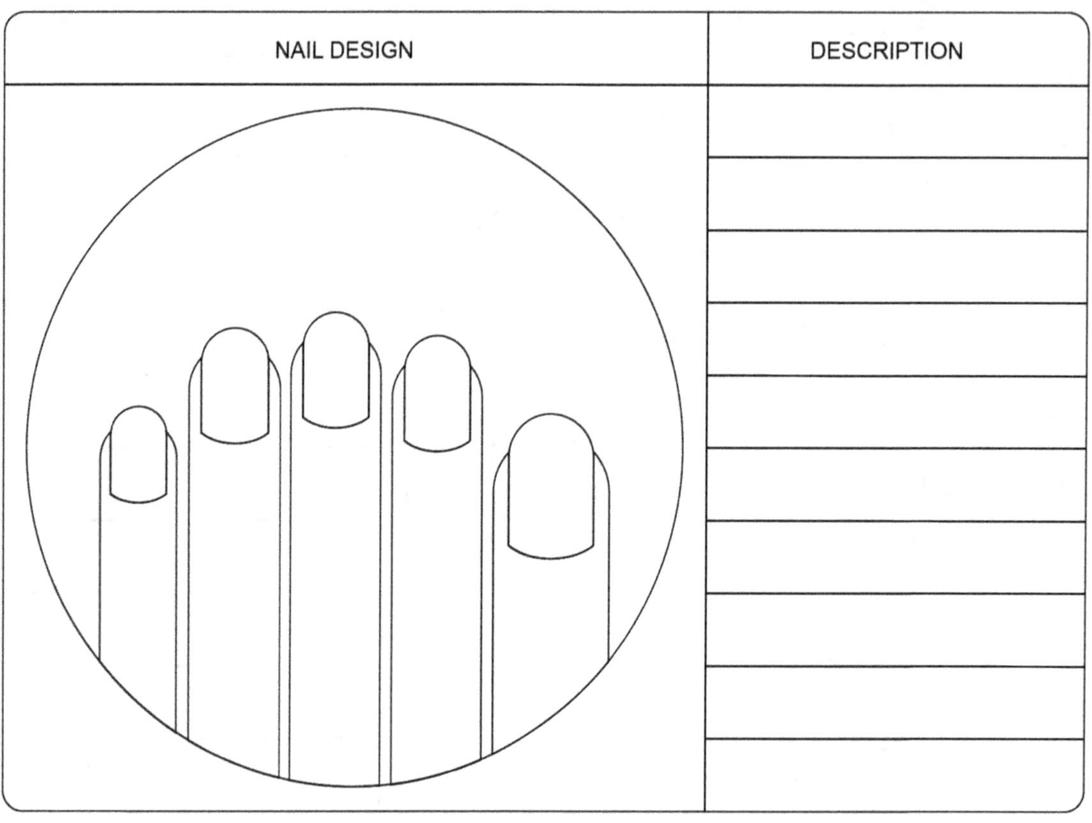	

COLOR PALETTE							
1	2	3	4	5	6	7	8

NR	COLOR	BRAND
1		
2		
3		
4		
5		
6		
7		
8		

DETAILS & PATTERNS

ADDITIONAL NOTES

DESIGN NAME .... DATE ....

NAIL DESIGN	DESCRIPTION
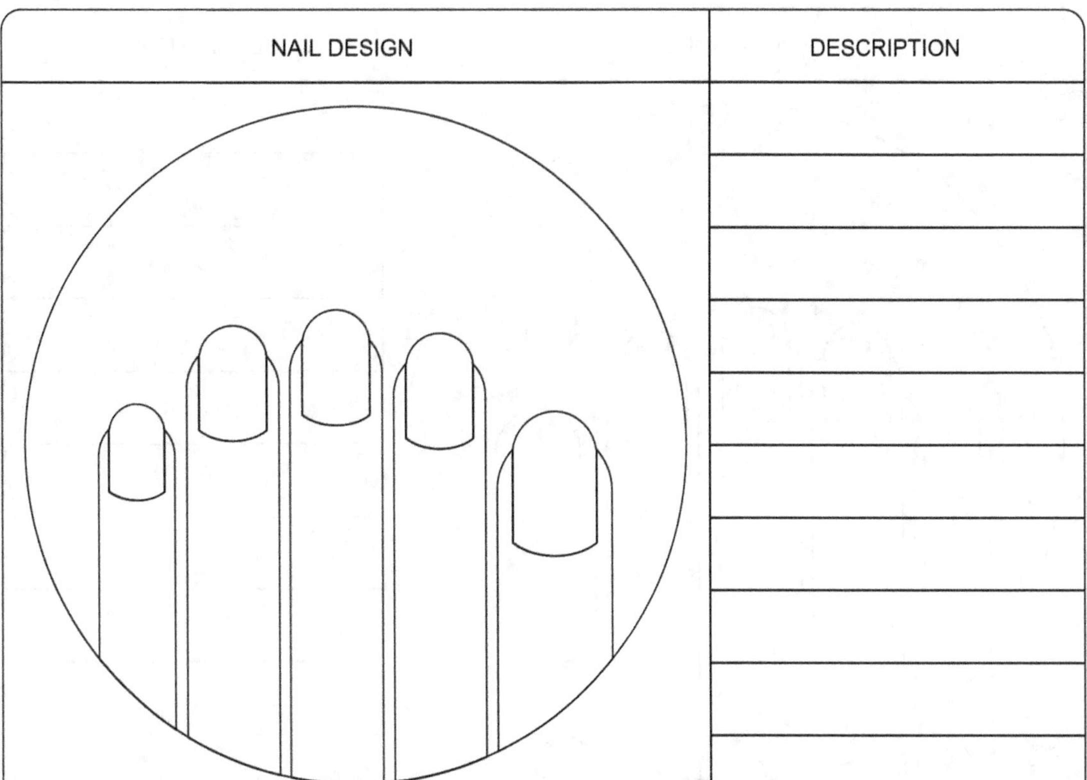	

COLOR PALETTE

1	2	3	4	5	6	7	8

NR	COLOR	BRAND
1		
2		
3		
4		
5		
6		
7		
8		

DETAILS & PATTERNS

ADDITIONAL NOTES

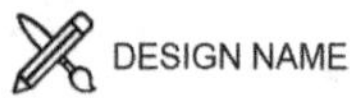

DESIGN NAME ....

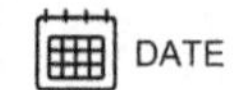

DATE ....

NAIL DESIGN	DESCRIPTION
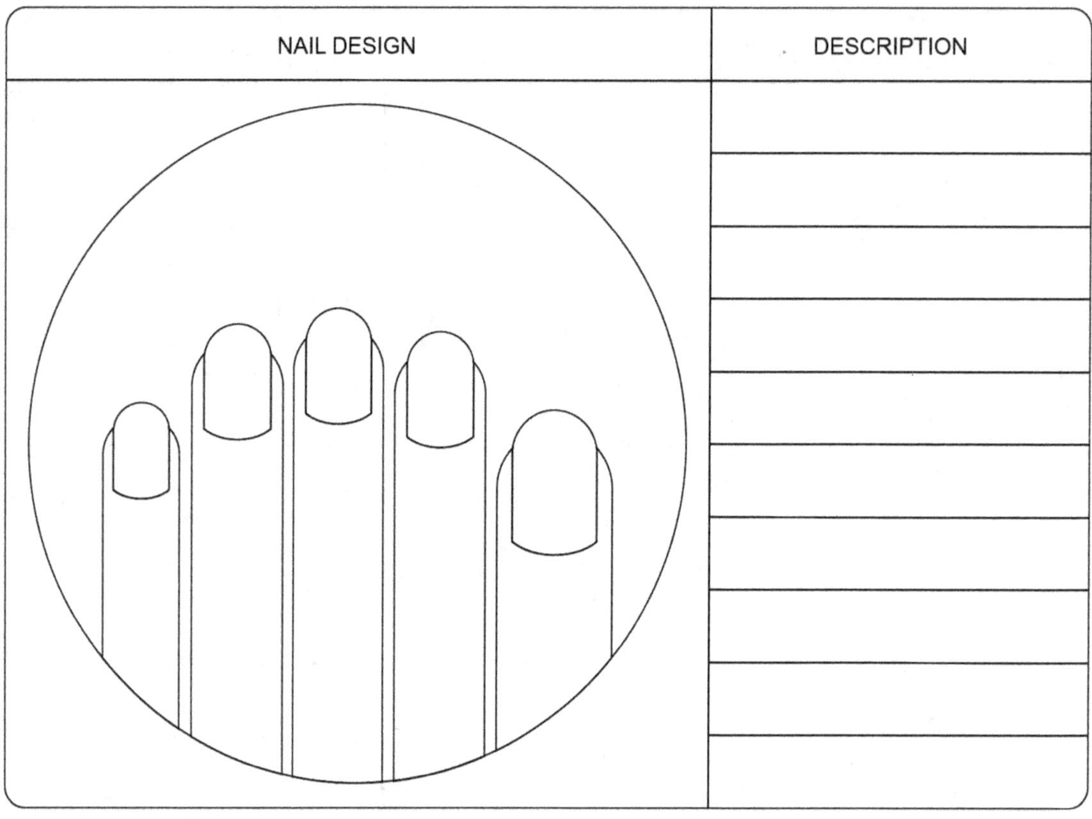	

COLOR PALETTE

1	2	3	4	5	6	7	8

NR	COLOR	BRAND
1		
2		
3		
4		
5		
6		
7		
8		

DETAILS & PATTERNS

ADDITIONAL NOTES

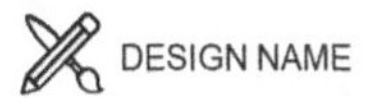
DESIGN NAME ....

DATE ....

NAIL DESIGN	DESCRIPTION
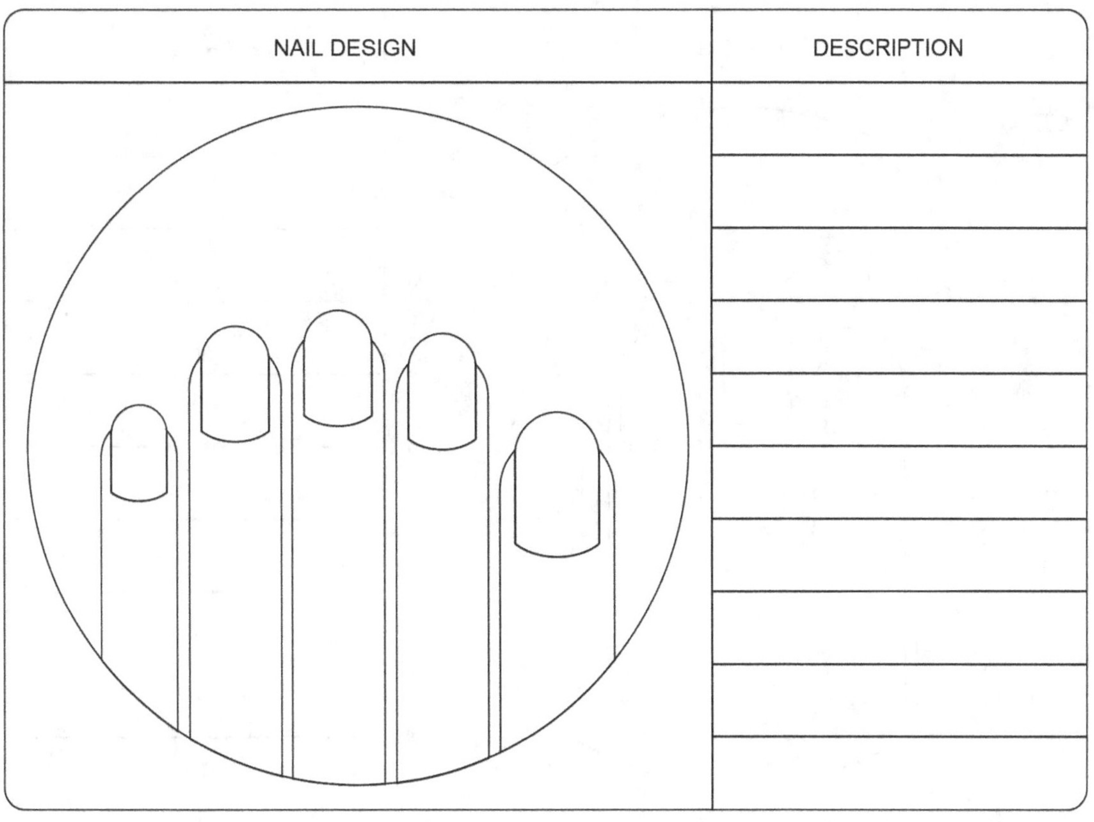	

COLOR PALETTE

1	2	3	4	5	6	7	8

NR	COLOR	BRAND
1		
2		
3		
4		
5		
6		
7		
8		

DETAILS & PATTERNS

ADDITIONAL NOTES

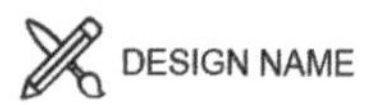

DATE ....

NAIL DESIGN	DESCRIPTION
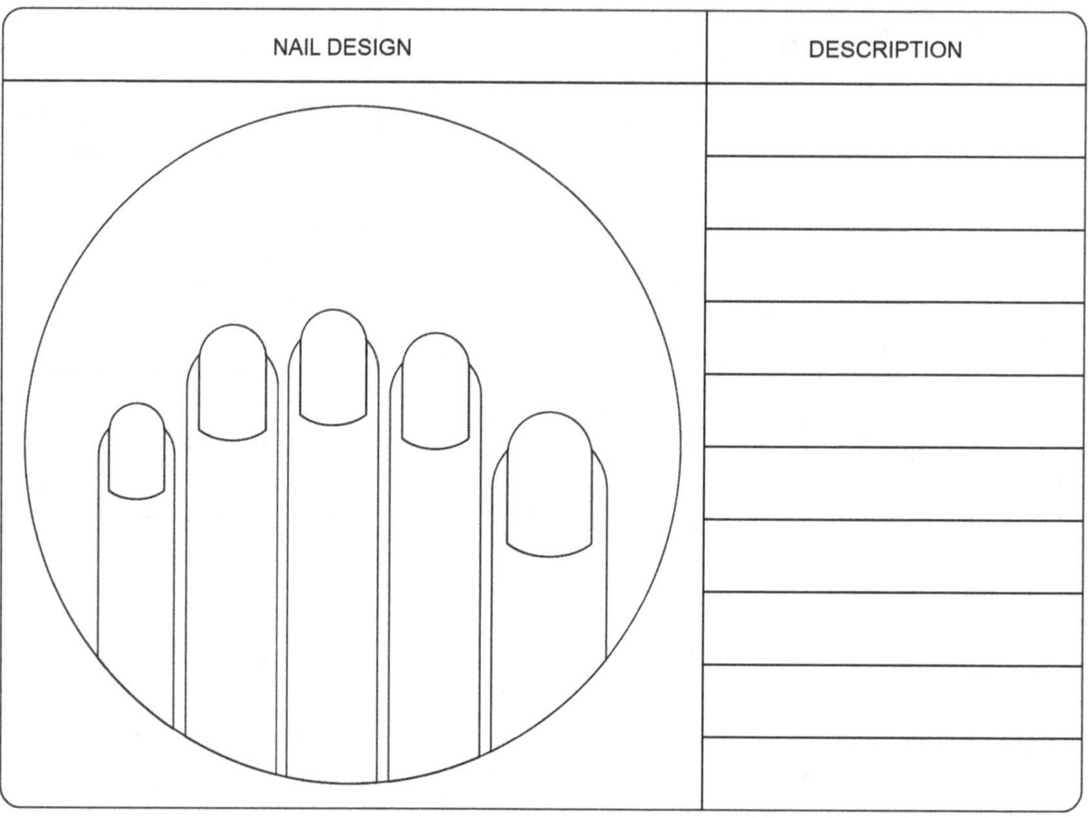	

COLOR PALETTE

1	2	3	4	5	6	7	8

NR	COLOR	BRAND
1		
2		
3		
4		
5		
6		
7		
8		

DETAILS & PATTERNS

ADDITIONAL NOTES

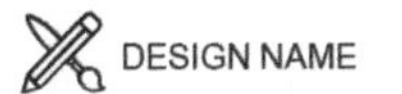
DESIGN NAME ....

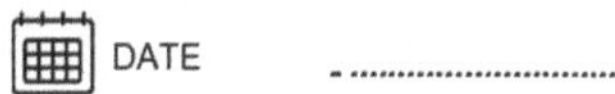
DATE ....

NAIL DESIGN	DESCRIPTION

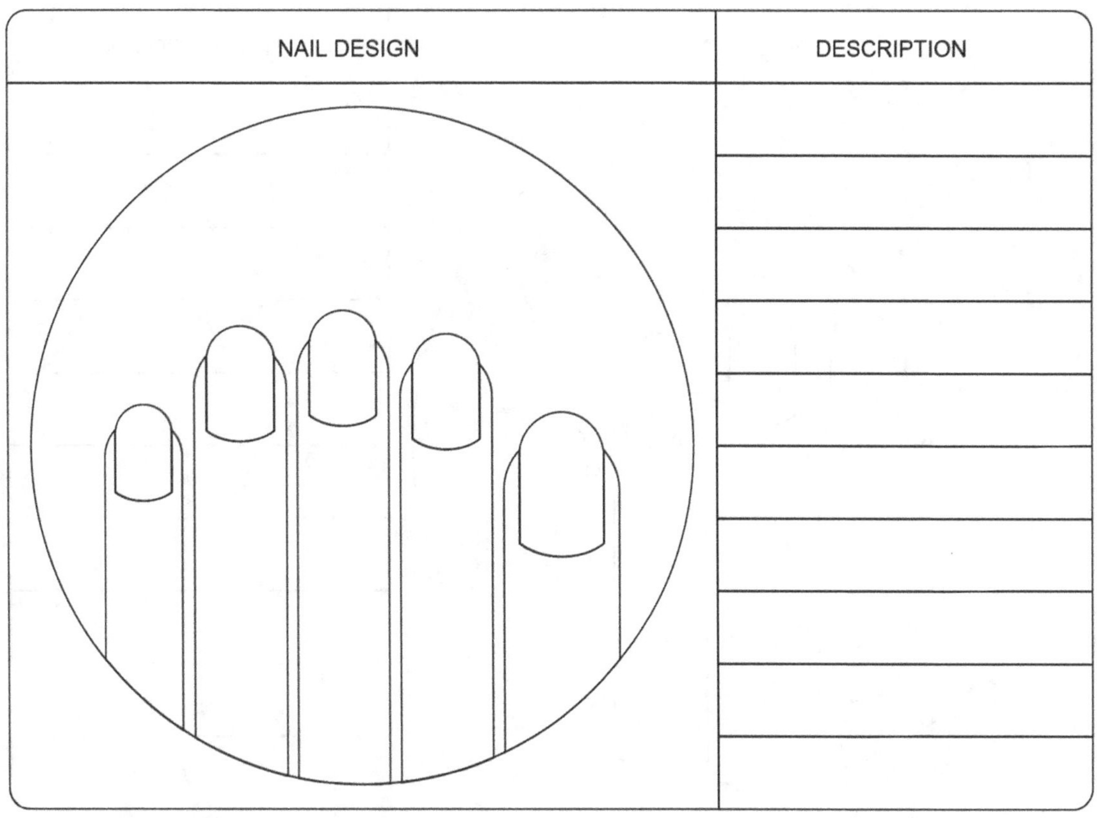

COLOR PALETTE

1	2	3	4	5	6	7	8

NR	COLOR	BRAND
1		
2		
3		
4		
5		
6		
7		
8		

DETAILS & PATTERNS

ADDITIONAL NOTES

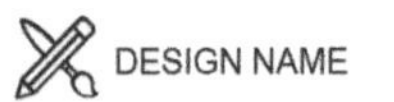

DESIGN NAME

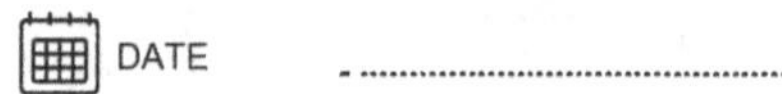

DATE

NAIL DESIGN	DESCRIPTION

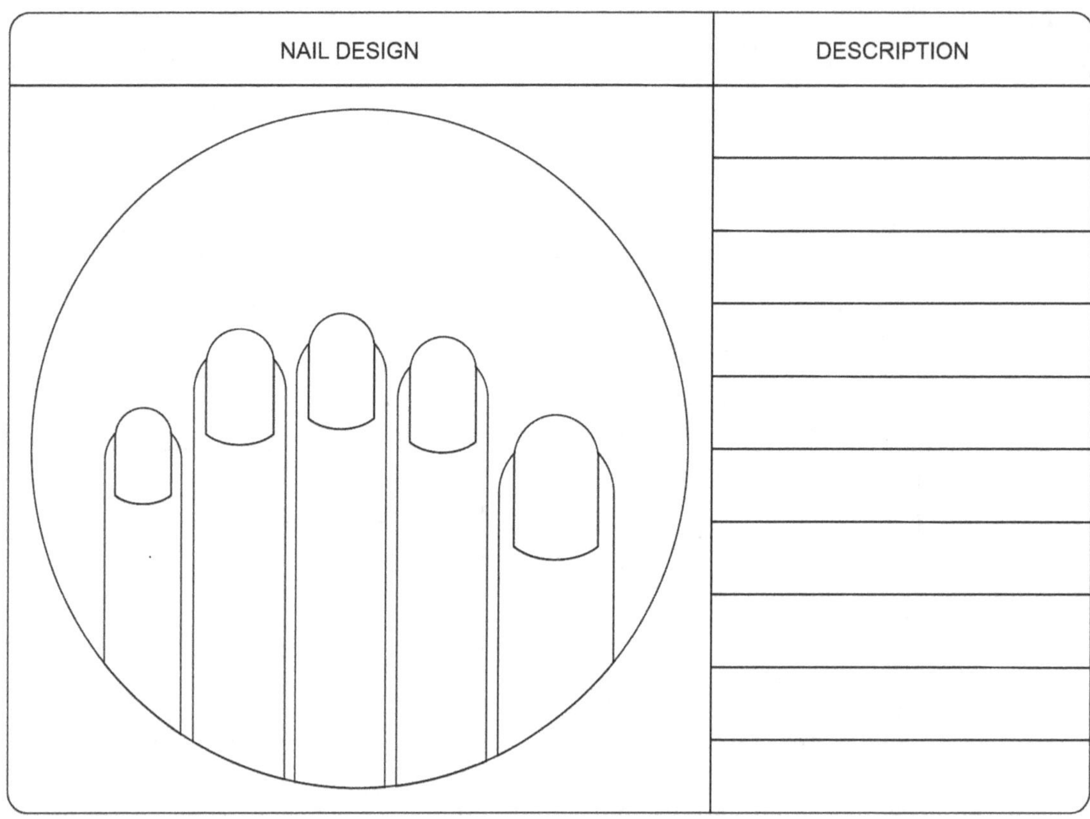

COLOR PALETTE

1	2	3	4	5	6	7	8

NR	COLOR	BRAND
1		
2		
3		
4		
5		
6		
7		
8		

DETAILS & PATTERNS

ADDITIONAL NOTES

www.ingramcontent.com/pod-product-compliance
Lightning Source LLC
Chambersburg PA
CBHW080400030726
47598CB00010B/2823

* 9 7 8 1 9 5 3 3 3 2 2 0 2 *